IN THE FOOTSTEPS O

A Journey through the Cevennes

Also by Alan Plowright

Plowright Follows Wainwright
Hot-Foot Through The Highlands
A Glimpse of Yorkshire
Another Glimpse of Yorkshire
Land's End to John O'Groats – In Fifteen Years!
Blind Jack
Rock Valley and Oddicroft Lane Recollections *
Memories of Tin Box Making in Mansfield & Sutton   *
John Henry's Walk

*

Compiled in conjunction with Alan Atkins

IN THE FOOTSTEPS OF STEVENSON

A Journey Through the Cévennes

Alan Plowright

Moorfield Press

First Published in Great Britain
by
Moorfield Press 2007

Copyright © Alan Plowright 2007

Page layout by
Highlight Type Bureau Ltd, Bradford, West Yorkshire
Printed in England by
The Amadeus Press, Cleckheaton, West Yorkshire

A CIP catalogue record for this book is available
from the British Library

ISBN 9780953011995

The moral right of the author has been asserted

Colour photographs : Alan Plowright
Cover Design: Corrina Korrubel
Maps and sketches: John W Holroyd

Contents

Introduction

The view through the classroom window to the imposing twin towers of Southwell Minster was one to be admired. I gazed unseeingly across its lush green churchyard, my thoughts elsewhere. In my mind's eye I was scaling the high Cévennes in the company of a stubborn donkey. The sun beat mercilessly upon us and my tortured limbs rebelled as I forced myself up the relentless slope, dragging my unwilling companion in my wake.

'Plowright!' Shaken from my reverie by the harsh interruption of the English master, I replied shamefacedly, 'Yes, sir?' He put down the copy of Robert Louis Stevenson's *Travels With a Donkey in the Cévennes* from which he had been reading. 'Am I boring you?' he inquired, amidst sniggers from my classmates. 'Oh no, sir!' I replied, 'I was listening to every word.' The master bristled as the laughter grew louder. 'Are you making fun of me, boy?' 'Not at all, sir,' I answered quickly, keen to assuage his anger, 'I was imagining myself in Stevenson's shoes.' A thin smile crossed his face. 'In that case, would you care to summarise the last passage I was reading?' To his surprise I described in detail Stevenson's surroundings during his testing climb up a rugged mountainside.

This event, in the dim and distant past of my schooldays, was one that I have never forgotten. That intriguing account of Stevenson's journey must have nurtured a desire to travel on foot, for in later life, when my children had grown up, I began to walk the hills and dales of Yorkshire, a prelude to many long-distance treks around Britain.

Recently, I re-read his narration of the walk, in 1878, from Le Monastier through the Cévennes to St. Jean du Gard, accompanied by a small grey donkey that carried his belongings reluctantly. The years rolled away as I pored over his account of their adventures. Once again, I became filled with an overwhelming desire to follow in his footsteps and discover how life has changed in that area of France over the intervening years.

Preface

The luxurious, verdant and once volcanic countryside of the Vélay flashed past the window of the train bound for Le Puy. As I pondered my forthcoming expedition of over one hundred and twenty miles I gazed unseeingly at this sea of green that was almost a blur. Momentarily, I found myself transported back to the period just after the Second World War when I had similarly looked fixedly from another window, that of my classroom, enthused by Stevenson's account of the journey I was about to undertake. I could scarcely believe that I was about to realise my long-held ambition and my heart missed a beat. Myriad questions tumbled through my mind. How would I fare in the heat of June? Would I succumb to exhaustion during the severest sections of the walk? How would I cope with the language of those I might meet in the remote settlements? My French had not been put to the test since leaving school.

Having studied Stevenson's background I knew that he would have had no such problem in conversing. Although born in Edinburgh, he made his first visit to France at the age of fourteen, where he spent the winter in Menton, a neighbour of Monte Carlo. His mother accompanied him, hoping that the warm and efficacious climate of the French Riviera would be good for his poor health which, unfortunately, was to remain for the rest of his short life. His serious chest problems culminated in tuberculosis, which resulted in his early death at the age of forty-four. Having become a serious traveller at a relatively young age and a dedicated, if initially unsuccessful writer, Stevenson began to spend increasing periods in France. He visited Paris and stayed for a time in the artistic colonies around Fontainebleau, on its outskirts, no doubt wishing to mix with like-minded writers and artists. It was here that the Barbizon school of French painting was established and the place where he met his wife-to-be, Fanny Osbourne, an American artist, separated from her husband and accompanied by two children. Drawn together by a common love of their artistic environment and lifestyle they fell in love and eventually married in San Francisco, in 1880, when Stevenson was thirty-one years old. Their honeymoon was spent in an abandoned bunkhouse at the disused Silverado mine on the slopes of Mount St. Helena, in California

Before their marriage, Stevenson explored the unrestrained hilly country of the Auvergne, set in the wilds of the north of the Massif Central, a land peppered with extinct volcanoes. This, I believe, resulted in a wish for further scrutiny to the south of this region and was the reason for him setting out from th` small town of Le Monastier in 1878, bound for St. Jean au Gard, with an obstinate donkey. Another probable reason for his journey was to gather material for a book about the experience. He had already entered the realms of travel writing with a book describing a canoe trip by canal and river, from Antwerp to Pontoise, a town situated to the north-west of Paris. Entitled *An Inland Voyage*, it was his first full-length publication. A further explanation for his trek is possibly the fact that Fanny Osbourne, who was still married to her first husband, had left suddenly for the United States to obtain a divorce and left Stevenson cooling his heels.

Whatever the reason his renowned phrase sums up his thoughts at that time. 'For my part, I travel not to go anywhere, but to go. I travel for travel's sake. The great affair is to move.' However, I am of the opinion that this was not his sole objective, for like any dedicated writer and traveller he would relish discovering new places and observing the countryside in all its moods. The artist within him must have appreciated nature in its varied forms and the landscapes that had been shaped by its dramatic workings.

These facets of Stevenson's remarkable life engaged my thoughts until the train was fast approaching Le Puy, my destination for the night. The usual excitement before the outset of a long walk began to build. What new people were about to enter my life? What would conditions be like on the journey? Probably much better than during Stevenson's traverse, I anticipated, for it has become the Robert Louis Stevenson Trail, now a designated Grande Randonnée, (European long-distance route) known as the GR 70. It is waymarked with the familiar red and white signs of the GR, which, I assumed, would make my route finding less arduous. I did not expect to be travelling alone, for the Trail is walked by people from many countries, including those on self-guided holidays operated by travel companies. Instead of the services of Stevenson's donkey, Modestine, for transportation of luggage, the latter can enjoy the onward movement of their main belongings by modern transport.

PART 1

(An account of Stevenson's journey in 1878)

Robert Louis Stevenson

Stevenson's Route

CHAPTER ONE

LE MONASTIER TO BOUCHET ST-NICHOLAS

Robert Louis Stevenson began his journey on the 22nd of September 1878, in what he describes as 'a little place called Monastier, in a pleasant highland valley.' He had spent a month there, probably acclimatising himself with the people and his surroundings. During this period he began sketching, an activity that he pursued throughout his expedition, in fact he made over twenty drawings of the area around Le Monastier.

Stevenson discovered that local conflicts flourished between the followers of the four French political parties of that time and also those brought about by drunkenness and freedom of language. He highlighted the loathing that many inhabitants had for their fellows, some never deigning to speak to each other except when business was at stake or to begin a tavern brawl.

Despite these animosities, Stevenson found the local people kind and helpful, somewhat due, he believed, to the mention of his forthcoming journey through the Cévennes, a rare event in those days. However, he was quick to point out that these mountain people displayed a natural hospitality, although they were puzzled by his need undertake a lone walk of over one hundred miles through mountainous country. Stevenson indicates that lone travellers are often looked upon as no better than thieves and vagabonds and in many quarters he was regarded with deep suspicion.

Autumn had arrived when Stevenson began his journey and he carried a waterproof sleeping sack in case he could not find accommodation. He was averse to taking a tent, which, he thought, was too irksome to pitch and the sack would also serve as a valise. Stevenson also did not wish to advertise the fact that he may be camping overnight, for 'if it is not secret it can be a troubled refuge, with unwelcome visitors.'

In order to carry the sack and its cargo of clothes it was necessary to obtain a beast of burden. 'What I required was something small and cheap, hardy and of a solid and

1

La Chapelle Saint-Jean, Le Monastier

peaceful temper; and all these requisites pointed to a donkey.' Consequently, he began a search for such an animal and he came across Modestine, owned by Father Adam a local man of rather limited intellect. Father Adam tried to demonstrate the donkey's placid nature by allowing a succession of children to ride her. Unfortunately, they all ended up in the dust of the market-place and the trial was terminated. A little later negotiations were recommenced, aided by a significant number of villagers and Stevenson was the centre of a commotion for around half an hour. Eventually, Modestine was purchased for sixty-five francs and a glass of brandy.

On the advice of a local saddler, a leather pad was made to go over Modestine's back and fitted with rings to secure Stevenson's load, which was significant. It consisted of a spirit lamp, pan, lantern, candles, jack-knife, an egg-whisk and a large leather flask. In addition there were two changes of warm clothing, travelling wear of country velveteen, pilot coat, knitted jacket, books and a railway rug. Provisions included chocolate cakes, tins of sausage, a leg of mutton, a

A Family Gathering

bottle of Beaujolais, an empty bottle to carry milk and a considerable amount of bread, black for the donkey and white for Stevenson. Quite a burden for poor Modestine.

On the day of his departure Stevenson rose shortly after 5am and before 6am he began to load Modestine, not an easy task, for the pack refused to stay in place. To counter this problem Stevenson had a pack-saddle fitted to the donkey's back and once again loaded her with the doubled sack and all his belongings. This activity was watched with relish by a gossiping crowd, that probably realised this tenderfoot traveller was inviting trouble. The elaborate system of knots and straps did not make for a sound attachment of the load and Stevenson left the village like a lamb to the slaughter.

It was 9am when Stevenson began his epic journey, the first section being twenty miles over rolling country to the village of Le Bouchet St. Nicholas. The peels of the church bells accompanied his departure.

After fording a stream the pair began to climb through pinewoods and, using the stick that he was carrying,

Stevenson urged Modestine to increase her pace. This ill-treatment was soon abandoned when he noticed that the donkey was quivering and breathing heavily. Consequently he had to stick to Modestine's modest pace and, unless he kept abreast of her, the donkey would stop and begin to graze.

A peasant overtook them and asked if they had travelled far, for he could not help but notice their slow pace. He laughed when told that they had barely left Le Monastier. The man plucked a shoot from a tree and laid about Modestine's haunches with it. Remarkably, the animal's pace quickened and was maintained. At that point, Stevenson realised that the crafty donkey had been playing him for a fool. Before they parted company the peasant gave the shoot to Stevenson, declaring that Modestine would feel it less harshly than the stick. 'Proot,' the man said, as he left. 'That is the word used by donkey drivers and it will serve you well.'

For the rest of the morning and through the afternoon, their new-found pace was kept up, much to Stevenson's satisfaction, and he was able to take in more of his surroundings. It being Sunday, the fields were devoid of workers and quietly basking in the sunshine. As they passed the church in St. Martin de Fugères Stevenson found it overflowing, some of the congregation even kneeling on the steps. The sound of the priest's voice within transported Stevenson to his homeland as he was an observer of the Sabbath. It also prompted him to issue the following time-honoured lines. 'It is only a traveller, hurrying by like a person from another planet, who can rightly enjoy the peace and beauty of the great ascetic feast. The sight of the resting country does his spirit good. There is something better than music in the wide unusual silence; and it disposes him to amiable thoughts, like the sound of a little river or the warmth of sunlight.'

So it was that Stevenson was in good humour as he descended the valley in which nestles Goudet. Through the green and lush defile runs the infant Loire, overlooked on all sides by imposing mountains. To Stevenson it seemed a veritable Shangri-La, cut off from civilisation, with only rocky footpaths linking Goudet to the outside world.

After a hurried lunch-stop at the Hotel de Loire Stevenson crossed the burgeoning waters of the Loire and began to climb the testing slope on the far side of the valley. Modestine reverted to her unyielding and dilatory self, refusing to respond to innumerable 'Proots.' Stevenson began to despair of reaching Lac Bouchet, their destination for the night, where he intended to set up camp. In his frustration he began to beat the stubborn donkey, but was racked with guilt by her resemblance to a lady of his acquaintance who had shown him nothing but kindness.

To compound Stevenson's discomfort, they met a male donkey grazing at the roadside and Modestine stopped to greet him enthusiastically. In order to separate the love-birds, Stevenson began to lay about them with his stick and it was small wonder that Modestine's new-found companion did not attack him. Eventually, Stevenson was able to drag Modestine away and force her along the road, with sweat pouring from him. His tribulations did not end there, for at regular intervals Modestine's load slipped to one side or the other. Having just managed to extract a reasonable pace from the animal he was forced to keep stopping and struggle to right the load.

This performance carried on until they reached the village of Ussel, whereupon saddle, load and all slipped completely round Modestine's body and dangled in the dust of the road. Several villagers, attracted by the entertaining sight, gathered round waiting for the next episode, which was not long in coming. Completely unaided by his audience, during a strength-sapping struggle, Stevenson managed to right the load once more. However, his satisfaction was short-lived, for it immediately slipped over in the other direction. One of the villagers declared that his sack should be a different shape, which caused Stevenson to all but tell him to mind his own business.

Stevenson's solution to the problem was to split Modestine's load and carry a fair proportion in each hand. As he struggled through the village, the obstructive animal tried to enter every house and courtyard, as though conscious that her master had no hand with which to

Sketch of Château Beaufort by Stevenson

restrain her.

A priest and some of his flock were surveying a church that was under repair and when they saw the antics of the passing Stevenson and Modestine they burst into laughter, which did not improve his temper.

As they left the village, Modestine set off along a by-road, refusing to be diverted and Stevenson, in his frustration, struck her twice across the face. Horrified by his cruel action, Stevenson sat down by the roadside and produced his pipe and brandy, hoping that a rest and some stimulation would enable him to gather his thoughts. As he pondered, Modestine chewed nonchalantly on some black bread. It was plain that drastic action was needed and he must lighten his load. Consequently, Stevenson discarded the bottle intended for carrying milk, the leg of mutton, the white bread and the egg whisk. He kept the remains of the black bread for the donkey.

When they recommenced their journey, Stevenson now had one hand free, with which he began to beat Modestine, urging her on in order to reach the lake before dark. The sun was already sinking into creeping mist, the temperature was dropping and the route became difficult to follow along a confusing network of by-roads. Despite being able to see the peak that overlooked his destination, the roads seemed to take him no closer to it. In his despondency, the stick became very active on Modestine's haunches, in fact it made the only sound in that rapidly darkening wilderness. Suddenly the load capsized once more, scattering his possessions on the road. This tragedy cost a valuable half-hour, whilst Stevenson re-packed the load, using an improved system, by which time it was all but dark.

Reaching a wasteland of turf and stones, Stevenson saw two shadowy figures approaching at a good pace. They turned out to be mother and son, the lady being decked out in her Sunday best. As they reached Stevenson he heard the mother issue a string of lewd oaths, quite at odds with her appearance. Instead of stopping, the couple walked past quickly, ignoring Stevenson's beckoning cry. Desperate for guidance, Stevenson ran after them and implored them to point the way to Lac Bouchet. The mother asked why he

Modestine refuses to move

wished to go there at that late hour, but Stevenson met her question with an inquiry as to how far they had to go that evening. Letting out another oath she replied that another hour and a half's toil awaited them and that he should follow them to the lake.

The couple strode on without further discussion into the gathering gloom and Stevenson, urging on Modestine, followed hurriedly. Soon they reached a high road and Stevenson was surprised to find the village of Bouchet St. Nicholas nearby. He had been informed that the area around the lake was unoccupied. Leaving his companions to their march, Stevenson entered the village and made for the inn, having abandoned the idea of spending the night in the open air.

The inn at Bouchet St. Nicholas was quite austere and, as Stevenson was to discover, typical of many inns in that part of France. It was little more than a cottage, with its stable and kitchen adjacent. The floors were earthen and there was a single bedchamber for travellers, housing nothing more

Calamity!

than beds. Meals were eaten in the kitchen and the family also slept there. Washing was a communal affair at the kitchen table. He found the food, both there and at subsequent inns, often sparse. Hard fish and omelette were common, the wine in short supply and the brandy, terrible. At mealtimes a fat sow could often be found under the table rubbing against the legs of the diners whilst rummaging for scraps.

Despite the basic accommodation, Stevenson found the majority of innkeepers and their families to be kind and considerate. In contrast to his problem with the unfriendly couple that had guided him to the village he generally found the country people, when at home, to be quite the opposite.

During a meal at the inn, Stevenson was obliged to use his own knife, as was common in those times. His jack-knife, with its spring was highly acclaimed by the landlord, who would take very little of Stevenson's proffered Beaujolais in case he was not leaving enough for his benefactor.

The landlord's wife, who appeared to rule the household, grilled Stevenson about his journey. When she learned that he intended to write a book concerning his trek she indicated quickly and accurately what information he was likely to put in it. 'You will tell of the beauties of Nature and if there are forests. Also of peasants' routines on the farms, people's manners, and what is told to you by folk such as my husband and me.'

The landlord, although uneducated and rustic, was very concerned to hear of Stevenson's tribulations with Modestine. He promised to provide a much-improved means of controlling her on the following morning. 'You could beat her with a cudgel and still arrive nowhere,' he indicated.

Stevenson spent an uncomfortable night's rest. The cause being the proximity of a young family occupying the adjacent bed; a cooper from Alais, travelling with his wife and child to St. Etienne to find work. To cover his embarrassment, Stevenson offered the man a conciliatory drink of brandy from his flask. This caused him to believe that Stevenson was a brandy merchant.

CHAPTER TWO

BOUCHET ST-NICHOLAS TO LANGOGNE

Rising early on the following morning, Stevenson washed hurriedly, drank a bowl of milk and left the inn to survey the locality. He walked briskly, for the morning was cold and wintry and although it was yet 5am villagers were already making their way to the fields to begin their day's toil. Many heads turned to stare at the stranger in their midst.

Returning to the inn for breakfast, Stevenson came upon the landlord's wife, who told him that her husband was busy making a goad. He was keeping his promise of the previous evening and a little later presented Stevenson with a wand having a pin protruding from the business end. It proved a godsend, for Stevenson had merely to jab Modestine none too roughly to make her more fleet of foot.

His journey to Pradelles was lonely on that bitterly cold morning. He met no one, apart from a group of ladies, a pair of postmen and an inquisitive foal that ran up to him, before scurrying away as quickly as it had arrived.

He found it an old and attractive little town having an arcaded market square with a distinctly Spanish appearance. It perched on a hillside far above the River Allier amidst lush meadows. It was once fortified and contained an array of venerable houses lining its narrow streets.

All around hay was being cut and gathered, giving rise to an all-pervading scent of the fields. On the opposite side of the valley steep slopes stretched for what seemed miles to meet the cheerless sky. Narrow roads threaded the autumn landscape that despite its pallid countenance was stimulating to Stevenson. He had reached the southern extremity of the Vélay and another county lay before him; that of untamed Gévaudan, rugged, barren and recently de-forested through fear of wolves.

Through his thirst for adventure, Stevenson bemoaned the absence of wolves on his journey, but I am unsure of his reaction if confronted by one. It was obvious that he carried a revolver for just such an occurrence.

11

Langogne

Gévaudan, he relates, was the land of the unforgettable 'beast,' which, according to folklore was a king among wolves that ate children and beautiful shepherdesses. It was reputed to have pursued armed horsemen, post-chaises and outriders along the highway. The 'beast' appeared on placards and ten thousand francs was offered for its head, yet when it was shot and taken to Versailles, it turned out to be nothing more than a small wolf. Despite this, it was remembered in song and made the hero of a novel.

Stevenson had a hurried lunch in a nearby inn, refusing the landlady's suggestion that he visited 'Our Lady of Pradelles,' who is reputed to perform many miracles, when he discovered she was made merely of wood.

He was soon on the road once more, goading Modestine down the steep descent, making for Langogne that lies on the Allier. On his route out of town he passed the church containing the image of 'Our Lady of Pradelles,' but did not linger. In the surrounding fields farmers toiled at the plough, busily preparing the soil for spring sowing and

Two Couples!

creating a fine dust that travelled on the wind. Stevenson described his surroundings as 'a fine, busy, breathing, rustic landscape.'

As he continued his descent, the approaching hills of Gévaudan began to blot out the sky and in the valley bottom he entered Langogne, an old established town, that lay on the northern fringe of Languedoc. He found much of historical interest, including several degraded towers, the Tour de l'Horloge, a medieval gateway and a twelfth-century church with a fifteenth-century façade.

After partaking of some refreshment at the Bel Air Hotel he collected Modestine and continued his day's journey. Down in the valley bottom he crossed the bridge spanning the River Allier, a close neighbour of the River Loire. As he did so he was accosted by a young girl, who asked where he was going in an extremely haughty manner. The question, from the mouth of a child no older than eight, caused Stevenson to burst into laughter. She could only stare at him angrily as he passed her without a word, so hard was he laughing as he entered Gévaudan.

He was kept amused by this incident as he searched the valley for a suitable place to set up camp. Eventually, he found a shaded spot and, after feeding Modestine and himself he settled down to sleep.

CHAPTER THREE

LANGOGNE TO FOUZILHAC

The following day it was past noon before Stevenson took to the road once more. The morning was spent repairing his empty knapsack that he had stowed in his sleeping sack as a contingency. This was used to transport some of his belongings, thus spreading the load and easing his progress.

Stevenson's next objective was the village of Le Cheylard l'Evêque and he was told by a local man that it was an hour and a half's walk away. He toiled up the demanding slope out of the fertile valley. In the higher reaches, marshy heather moors clothed much of the land, but the finer spectacle of birch woods, glowing yellow in the autumn light, were much in evidence. There being no direct road to Cheylard, Stevenson crossed hill and valley in driving rain and hail, attempting to negotiate a labyrinth of confusing tracks, until around 4pm he arrived at Sagne-Rousse. This provided a landmark on his route and gave him comfort that he was on course. Two hours later, at dusk, he emerged from an extensive pinewood hoping for sight of Cheylard, but an all but empty valley lay before him. This was a severe blow as nightfall was fast approaching. The only sign of relief was the ringing of cowbells that he had heard for quite sometime and ahead of him he caught sight of several cows and a ring of shadowy figures. As he approached them he noticed that the figures were those of children who were performing a kind of ritualistic dance, which Stevenson found eerie and strange on the marshy ground in the half-light. They were watched by a few onlookers who regarded him with suspicion and appeared reluctant to speak when Stevenson asked for directions. One old peasant hurried to his house and barricaded the door, whilst another man, who did deign to give Stevenson instructions, watched him begin to take the wrong course without a word of correction. Two of the dancing girls were even worse. One put her tongue out at him and the other suggested mockingly that he follow the cows that were now on the move. They both sniggered and

Ruined Chateau

dug each other in the ribs, which caused Stevenson to think of the 'Beast of Gévaudan' that had eaten, reputedly, about a hundred children of the district. What a pity it could not have eaten those two urchins, he thought maliciously!

He made a resentful departure, goading and guiding Modestine along a track until they reached another area of turf and heather. The brute of a donkey began to go round in circles and it took all Stevenson's strength to keep her on a straight course. Eventually he reached an easily discernable road and, as darkness was falling rapidly, Modestine sensed this and quickened her pace. As if to compound their woes the wind strengthened and it began to rain. To redress the balance some lighted windows in the hamlet of Fouzilhic hove into view. A tiny settlement consisting of three houses it clung to a hillside and here Stevenson received his first hint of kindness in Gévaudan. An old man left his dwelling and accompanied him for a short time, despite the rain, to put him on the road to Cheylard, refusing Stevenson's offer of recompense.

All seemed well until the night became suddenly pitch

A Shoeing Frame

black and Stevenson was unable to see an arm's length in front of him. His misery increased when the road split into several directions. Which road to take? He decided to try Modestine's intuition, but she began to wander around in circles and proved to be of no use whatsoever. Thinking that this short stage of his journey would be trouble-free, Stevenson had unfortunately not procured any food or wine, which did not make for a comfortable night's camp. The only sustenance he possessed was a tin of Bologna sausage some black bread and chocolate. If he could have found water he would have camped despite his hunger, but it would have been hard to find on that dark night. Stevenson decided to return to Fouzilhic and ask for further directions, but this was to prove far from simple. Shortly after turning round he lost the road and staggered over boggy open country only to find his way often barred by walls that Modestine could not scale.

At last he came within sight of lighted windows, only to plunge knee-deep into a bog. Despite his discomfort, relief flooded through him until he entered the hamlet and discovered that it was Fouzilhac and not Fouzilhic. Its inhabitants were not so kindly disposed as his helper in nearby Fouzilhic had been. At the first house he came to a woman refused to open the door and at the next a whole family appeared in the doorway holding lanterns. The husband refused point blank to cross the threshold and inquired as to Stevenson's destination beyond Cheylard. 'That is no affair of yours,' responded Stevenson indignantly. 'I need help and if you will not guide me yourself, at least help me to find someone else who will.' Instead of replying the man asked if Stevenson had passed the cows and the dancing children earlier that evening. At this point one of the girls that had been so rude to Stevenson spoke. He had not recognised her in the doorway and she confirmed to her father that it was he that had passed by. 'Why are you still here?' demanded the man, to which Stevenson replied that he would like to be away from the place if only the man would guide him. 'I will not cross the door!' cried the man, as though terror-stricken. Stevenson pulled himself up to his full height. 'Then, sir, you are a coward,' he said and turned his back on the family who retreated indoors. When the door had closed, Stevenson heard the sound of laughter and muttered to himself, 'the Beasts of Gévaudan!'

Having been dazzled by the lanterns, Stevenson could hardly see in the inky blackness of that disturbing night and he stumbled amongst rubbish heaps and stones to knock on the door of other houses. No one would answer his knocking. Cursing the unfriendly inhabitants of Fouzilhac, Stevenson left the village. Thankfully, the rain had stopped and the wind was beginning to dry his clothes, which persuaded him that he must camp overnight even without water or food. His immediate task was to find Modestine who he had tied to a gate before entering the village. After groping in the dark for around twenty minutes and falling once more into a bog, Stevenson found his companion and went in search of the sheltering confines of a wood. It was a further hour before he found a protective arch of tree branches that formed a veritable cave.

He found the spirit lamp, which lit at the second attempt

and gave half the remains of the black bread to Modestine, saving the other half for her breakfast. For his supper he chewed on the sausages and chocolate, eating them together like bread and meat. Rounding off his sparse meal with a welcome cigarette, he enjoyed one of his best ever smokes. Eventually, he snuggled into his fleece-lined sleeping sack, despite its mixed contents, placed his pistol to hand and settled down to sleep. The energetic wind provided a lullaby as he gradually drifted into slumber.

CHAPTER FOUR

FOUZILHAC TO LUC

Stevenson woke as dawn was breaking to find the wind still rustling the surrounding foliage and the road threading temptingly into the distance. He discovered that he was on the edge of a birch wood, with another of fir behind it. In the other direction the ground descended into a shallow green valley.

After pulling on his boots and gaiters, Stevenson approached Modestine, who was waiting patiently, tethered to a beech tree. He gave the donkey the last of the black bread before taking in more of his surroundings, which he found most stimulating. It seemed part of a grand adventure, being he knew not where and what the day would bring. Encircling bare hilltops lay under a morning sky flecked with wispy and scudding clouds. The air was biting cold, arousing pangs of hunger, so he chewed on the last of the chocolate and washed it down with slug of neat brandy.

One cigarette later, Stevenson collected his sack and stowed it on Modestine's saddle before the pair took their first steps of the morning. Thankfully, the brisk wind was at their backs, urging them on and suddenly, as they rounded a corner, Fouzilhic re-appeared. In addition, the old man who had escorted Stevenson for a little way on the previous evening came running from his house, hands raised in horror.

When Stevenson informed him of the previous night's misfortune the man wrung his hands in dismay, horrified that he had left him prematurely. Determined to make amends the old man accompanied Stevenson for a mile, limping alongside him until he was within striking distance of Cheylard. Having followed a roughly south-westerly route from Langogne he had now changed direction and was walking eastwards.

However, the village that Stevenson had sought for so long proved unexciting. It was a scattered place with a few humble dwellings and several open areas piled high with logs and faggots. Two tired-looking crosses leant listlessly at an angle as though ready to collapse. In the small and shambling church Stevenson found a signboard hanging like a banner, which displayed a few notices concerning activities in the village. He read that in 1877 the villagers donated forty-eight francs ten centimes to the 'Work of the Propogation of the Faith.' Stevenson hoped that a little of this money would be used to aid the country of his birth – possibly a halfpence for the poor souls of Edinburgh.

Calling at the local inn, Stevenson found it simple, but welcoming. All the furniture was in the kitchen, including beds, a cradle, and dining table. The good people who ran the establishment had five children, who were brought up in a God-fearing manner, and another was on the way. One of the children was kneeling at the foot of the stairs, engaged in morning prayers.

As Stevenson recounted his previous night's misadventure, the couple listened attentively and became most sympathetic. Apparently, the wood in which he had slept belonged to them and they seemed very concerned for his welfare. 'That despicable man who refused to give you guidance in Fouzilhac deserves arrest,' they said. 'Who knows what might have happened to you?'

When Stevenson downed thirstily more than a pint of milk the lady of the house was most perturbed and insisted that the remainder be boiled and sweetened with chocolate. His boots and gaiters were hung up to dry and when he attempted to write his journal, with it balanced on his knee, the eldest child let down a hinged table near the fireplace. Thus Stevenson was able to write in comfort, save from burning his legs on account of sitting so close to the fire. The table was thick with dust and the husband apologised, indicating that it was normally only used in winter. When his journal entry was complete Stevenson enjoyed an omelette and a mug of chocolate.

As he left the inn, Stevenson was accompanied by the husband, who explained that he had begun his working life as a mule handler and wished to examine Modestine. When he saw the load she was carrying he declared that it should be split into two, which would allow double the weight. Stevenson replied that the present weight was quite

Luc

sufficient and he had no intention of cutting his sleeping sack in two. 'It would lie more comfortably along each of her sides,' the man insisted. 'The single load makes her extremely tired.'

Upon close inspection, Stevenson found that Modestine's forelegs were red raw on the inside and blood was oozing from under her tail. Instead of sympathy, he felt only anger. Could the wretched mule not carry a sleeping sack and a few belongings? It brought *AEsop's Fable* to mind and the thought that he would end up carrying the donkey!

It was with a heavy heart that Stevenson continued the day's journey in an easterly direction on what had become a meandering route. His temper was not improved by a fierce wind that battered him so hard he was forced to hold onto the donkey's load with one hand all the way to Luc, his destination. A barren landscape served to deepen his wrath and he declared the countryside to be akin to the worst of the Scottish Highlands. In his foul temper he wondered why anyone would wish to visit Cheylard or Luc.

A Street Scene

Eventually, Stevenson emerged on a hilltop above the Allier once more and thought little of the unexciting vista that lay below him. Terraced hills surrounded the river, their lower slopes clothed with woods and fields and rising to bare or pine-covered peaks. He could see the ruined castle of Luc, its tower pointing skywards and, on a pinnacle, a tall white statue of 'Our Lady.' The village itself comprised two straggling rows of houses sandwiched between river and hillside, which Stevenson found uninspiring. Save for the remains of the castle, he could discern little of interest.

The inn, however, was impressive. It was spacious and well-kept. Similar to the inn at Cheylard, the kitchen housed two box-beds, in addition to a large stone fireplace topped by a lengthy chimney shelf holding lanterns and religious statuettes. This establishment boasted a public bedroom with three box beds, several long tables and benches, large enough for many guests. The landlady, a good-looking and silent old woman was equally imposing, clothed and hooded like a nun.

23

Unfortunately, the sleeping arrangements were not to Stevenson's liking, for he spent the night in one of the box beds in the public bedroom lying on straw, shivering and trying to stop his teeth from chattering. He longed for his sheepskin-lined sack and the lee of a wood.

CHAPTER FIVE

LUC TO CHASSERADÈS

The following morning Stevenson left the hotel with Modestine's load re-arranged. His sleeping sack, no longer doubled, hung at full length, almost six feet, across her saddle. He had taken some of the advice of the landlord at Cheylard in his attempt to make Modestine's burden more stable and manageable.

The day's route lay south, mainly along the valley of the Allier that was threaded by the only portion of railway in Gévaudan. This formed part of a projected line that was still under survey and construction and was planned to run to the newly built station at Mende. Stevenson could visualise the impact the railway would have on this secluded region – 'The desert is beleaguered. Now may some Languedocian Wordsworth turn the sonnet into *patois:* Mountains and vales and floods, heard ye that whistle?'

Languedocian refers to the people of the region of Languedoc, which Stevenson was entering. Its name recalls the medieval language of the South, the 'langue d'oc,' so-called because its word for 'yes' was 'oc.' It encompasses the southern section of the Massif Central that contains stunning landscapes and striking natural features. The Grande Causse at the southern end of the Massif Central is an extensive plateau of raised limestone pavements cut through by deep canyons, the Gorge du Tarn being the most spectacular. The Causse is a vast, thinly populated region, riddled with underground streams and cave systems. It was established in medieval times to provide a base for groups of knights employed to protect travellers. Noted for its rugged beauty, it boasts the haunted ruins of medieval castles, villages clinging tenaciously to cliffsides, strange rock formations and areas strewn with fantastically shaped blocks of granite.

Villages display the remains of these castles that were usually baronial dwellings rather than fortresses. Many other villages had grown up around the pilgrim churches. The centre of the region is crossed by one of the main pilgrim routes to Santiago de Compostela. Many of the

La Bastide in 1880

settlements catered for pilgrim traffic, offering both accommodation and the opportunity to pray at a local shrine.

Stevenson reached La Bastide Puylaurent without incident, where he was directed to leave the valley and follow a road that climbed the hills of the Ardeche towards his destination, the Trappist monastery of Notre Dame des Neiges (Our Lady of the Snows). The sun came out opportunely as he emerged from a wood to behold the wild reaches of Languedoc to the south. Towering hills, glowing like sapphire, bordered the horizon and nearer to hand rippled ridge after ridge, craggy and heather-strewn. The sun glistened on acres of bare rock with trees clothing the plunging hollows, a sight that that raised Stevenson's spirits – 'It was grateful to come, after so long, upon a scene of some attraction for the human heart.'

The scene at closer quarters was not so inspiring, but a cross marked the summit of every hill, signifying the proximity of the monastery to which Stevenson was heading. He quickened his step, eager to reach his target, until a white statue of the Virgin pointed the way to Our Lady of the Snows. Soon the clanging of a bell, carried on the wind, invaded his ears. For some unaccountable reason Stevenson's heart sank and he approached the monastery in abject terror, which he blamed on his Protestant upbringing. Slowly, he continued, like a person who had wandered into the universe of the departed, until he came upon a friar struggling with a barrowload of turf. The friar was clothed in white, which likened him to an apparition and his hood had slipped from his head revealing a completely bald and polished skull.

Stevenson was unsure how to approach this daunting individual. What was the etiquette when addressing a monk who obeyed a vow of silence, he wondered? Consequently, he doffed his cap and nodded to the friar, who, to Stevenson's great relief, also nodded and cheerfully addressed him. 'Was he visiting the monastery? Where was he from?' Stevenson replied that he did wish to visit and that he hailed from Scotland. The friar studied him earnestly before stating that he could not be a guest at Our Lady of the Snows, but he may get a meal before heading on his way. Realisation dawned that the friar thought he was a pedlar, so Stevenson explained that he was a traveller who intended to write a book and sketch the landscapes that he encountered. This had the desired effect on the monk who quickly changed his attitude and indicated that Stevenson must ask for the Father Prior and state his case to him. 'Tell him that Father Apollinaris has sent you,' he added.

When they drew close to the monastery gates, Father Apollinaris told Stevenson that he could not speak once he went inside its confines and that he would not enter with him. 'Try to see me as you leave,' he requested, before crying, 'I must not speak! I must not speak!' and dashing away from the monastery gates.

This show of eccentricity re-ignited Stevenson's fears, but he shrugged them off and passed through the entrance as fast as Modestine would allow. She appeared reluctant to enter the holy portals, which was unusual for her, for she normally tried to enter every gateway they came upon.

Our Lady of the Snows as Stevenson would have seen it

Father Michael, the Father Hospitaller, came to the gate, accompanied by two brown-robed brethren. They began to question Stevenson about his unusual pack, which seemed a considerable attraction for them. When they had examined it eagerly they asked him to follow them. Modestine was led to the stables and Stevenson, complete with pack, was received into the monastery and made welcome. He was taken to the pantry by Father Michael, a pleasant, cheerful soul, and given a glass of liqueur. Whilst Stevenson related his experiences so far on his journey, the good father listened politely, but in a rather detached fashion.

His drink completed, Stevenson was left on his own in the monastery garden, laid out in the main courtyard with a fountain and a statue of the Virgin surrounded by beds of multi-coloured dahlias. The surrounding buildings seemed rather bleak and unseasoned by time and weather, the only notable features being a belfry and two slated gables. Brown -robed and white-robed brethren walked silently along the paths and three of them knelt on a terrace, deep in prayer.

A Brother Feeding Hens

Stevenson felt chilled by the bleak surroundings and wondered how the monks fared during the inclement months when snow fell intermittently between October and May.

After a hearty meal, Brother Ambrose led Stevenson to a small, but clean guest room. All brothers who waited on visitors to the monastery were allowed to speak, and this particular one proved very talkative. The tiny room had whitewashed walls, was sparsely furnished and contained several religious objects, such as a crucifix and a bust of the late Pope. Stevenson found some good reading matter, for there were several books to hand. There was also a list of regulations for visitors, containing instructions concerning the services they should attend, when to meditate and when to rise and to retire. A footnote added 'Time should be spent examining your conscience and making good resolutions.'

Whilst Stevenson was dwelling on the regulations, Brother Ambrose returned with an Irish boarder, a deacon who had dwelt for seven years in retreat at a convent in

Belgium, followed by five years at Our Lady of the Snows. The man seemed delighted to see a Scotsman and was eager for news, having spent five years in the company of silent brethren. In return he offered his services as a guide to the monastery.

The Irishman took Stevenson to his room and showed him his few possessions that included the *Waverley Novels* and a book containing the Divine Office for each day, which, he assured Stevenson, was dutifully recited. He then took Stevenson on a tour of the cloisters, chapter house, vestry and workshops, explaining that each brother could choose his occupation, in addition to his religious duties and general labours. Singing in the choir was expected if he had an ear for music, but in his private hours he could engage in whatever activity he wished. The Irishman indicated that one brother studied literature, whilst Father Apollinaris was engaged in road-making and the Abbot bound books. In the workshops, Stevenson found brothers baking bread, making cartwheels, indulging in photography and even tending a gallery of rabbits.

The brethren were fasting, a regime which lasted from September to Easter when they were allowed but one meal per day and that was meagre. Despite this deprivation the monks displayed a cheerful and friendly countenance. 'A happier nor a healthier company I should scarce suppose that I have ever seen,' declared Stevenson.

In spite of being a heretic, Stevenson found the Trappist order appealing and a model of wisdom. A lengthy novitiate and a display of dedication are required before entrance to the order is granted. These are a prerequisite for the long days spent in prayer and toil. From 2am, when the bell sounds until 8pm, a monk's life is never leisurely. For example, the brother who keeps rabbits hurries from his hutches to the chapel, the chapter house or the refectory many times each day and in addition every hour he has an office to recite and a task to carry out.

At night, together with his Irish companion, Stevenson attended the gallery to observe the last hour of daily prayer and hear *Salve Regina*, recited after Divine Office, which brought the brethren's day to a close. The image of the whitewashed chapel, the strong manly voices raised in song and the silence during prayers became imprinted in Stevenson's mind. At the sound of the bell denoting the completion of the last Office and the arrival of the time for sleep he would hurry into the courtyard, his thoughts tumbling and awry. In his tiny room he would read for a while to calm his thoughts before sleep came to him.

During his stay at Our Lady of the Snows, Stevenson's heretical views landed him in trouble. This came about through his discussions with two fellow boarders, a priest and a former soldier. The country priest had travelled that morning from his parish near Mende to partake of four days of privacy and prayer. Opposite in all respects to the priest, the old soldier, who had risen to high rank, had the brisk authoritative air of a long-serving officer. Their discourse took place over supper and all went well whilst the topic was politics. However, when Stevenson referred later to Gambetta's moderation, the old soldier became exceedingly angry and challenged him to justify such a statement. When he noticed a warning look on the face of the priest, the soldier calmed down and the conversation ended.

Things came to a head once more on the following morning, over coffee, when the priest and the soldier discovered that Stevenson was a heretic. The two men displayed their narrow-mindedness by insisting that Stevenson had been led to the monastery by God and must change his views. Stevenson pleaded family beliefs as the reason for his stance on religion, but this failed to impress. 'Your mother and father are to blame?' ranted the priest. 'Then you must convert them when you return home!' Stevenson suggested that irrespective of different religions, the way to God was the same in the end. This provoked a tirade concerning Hell and damnation from the priest and the insistence that Stevenson should go to the Abbot and confess

Later, at dinner Stevenson was harangued once more by the priest until he lost patience and heartily protested at his treatment. The priest was mollified. He tried to assure Stevenson that he only had interest in saving his soul.

After dinner Stevenson loaded Modestine once more to recommence their journey. The evening was calm and the

Stevenson at the inn in Chasseradès

sky uncluttered as they left Our Lady of the Snows accompanied by the Irishman who walked with them for a short time. A little way from the monastery they came upon Father Apollinaris who took a break from road-building to go with them for a few hundred yards, whereupon Stevenson's companions shook his hand and wished him well. As they said their farewells Stevenson felt both elation and sadness. He regretted leaving his friends, but was filled with the anticipation of one who begins a new episode in his adventures.

Stevenson rejoined the infant Allier and headed towards its sources in the forest of Mercoire. When he left the river it was little more than a stream, having only recently begun its life in the hills of Gévaudan. A short climb over the crest of a mount and the traverse of a bare plateau brought him within reach of Chasseradès as the sun was setting. He was soon within its confines searching for the inn, which he found quickly.

His fellow guests that night were employed on a survey

of one of the planned railways of the region. They made bright and sociable companions and the future of France was discussed over many glasses of wine until they took to their beds at a late hour. There were too many guests for the four beds in the small upstairs room, but Stevenson was given a bed to himself whilst the others had to share.

CHAPTER SIX

CHASSERADÈS TO THE FOOT OF MONT LOZÈRE

Stevenson was awakened the following morning at 5am by an early morning call to his companions. Dawn was breaking on what promised to be a fine day and Stevenson dressed hurriedly and went downstairs for an early breakfast with the surveyors.

He was soon underway once more in bright sunshine, savouring his sun-kissed surroundings as he continued across the plateau and descended the steep-sided valley of the Chassezac. The gully was speckled with tiny hamlets, their presence revealed by smoke curling from their chimneys. Lush meadows, spiked with colourful broom, bordered the rivulet that threaded through a seemingly timeless valley. The evocative sound of a horn drifted over the landscape and he was later to discover that it belonged to a peasant leading his flock through the upland fields.

Stevenson crossed a bridge over the Chassezac and began a climb from the deep hollow, studying the path before him that wound upwards to the little settlement of L'Estampe. This was reached by way of steeply angled fields and sheltering woods of birch and beech, until he stood stranded at the end of its narrow street. His progress was blocked by a multitude of sheep, bleating in unison and the bells around their necks ringing in accompaniment. Eventually, a passage was cleared and Stevenson passed through the village before climbing the higher mountainous slopes of La Goulet. He encountered two men in a tree hacking away with pruning hooks, whilst singing lustily. As he threaded a birch wood, a little farther on, the sound of a flute and crowing cocks drifted on the air, which served to increase Stevenson's appreciation of his rustic and remote surroundings. The simple country people appeared happy in their daily tasks and uncomplaining of their demanding existence.

In his high spirits Stevenson decided to take a short cut. The steep narrow road he was following snaked up the hillside in a broad curve. To save time and distance, he decided to leave the road and rejoin it farther up the valley, but he had reckoned without Modestine. No sooner were they negotiating a grassy slope through dwarf woods than she reared violently, braying loudly, which came as a surprise for she had made very little sound until that stage. She nearly fell backwards as Stevenson repeatedly jabbed her with the goad. Determined to carry on, Stevenson persisted until Modestine began to climb once more and they eventually reached their goal, with Stevenson soaked in sweat.

There was no road over the summit of La Goulet, merely upright stones at intervals to guide the drovers. However, the grass underfoot was soft and bouncy, providing a convenient blanket on which to walk and it also provided a sweet scent. With only birds for company Stevenson crossed the mountain-top and on his decent towards Le Bleymard met a solitary traveller with a bullock cart. Across the valley he could see the Mont Lozère range, stark against the horizon, its summit ridge level and unspectacular.

His approach to Bleymard was memorable only for the sight of the high road from Villefort to Mende as it crossed a series of green meadows, from which emanated the melodic sounds of cowbells.

In Bleymard Stevenson found an inn in which he partook of a meal, but did not stay the night. Instead he set out to climb the foothills of the Lozère by way of a rough drove-road. Several peasants emerged from the surrounding woods, their bullock carts laden with pine trees for winter fuel.

Eventually, he left the road and followed a path through the pines to a clearing where he decided to set up camp. His campsite was carpeted with soft turf that would provide an amenable bed and water was to hand in the form of a tiny stream that tumbled merrily over stones. A thick belt of trees surrounded the glade, creating a secure and private shelter, an ideal spot for a night under the stars.

Stevenson laid out his sleeping sack, fed Modestine and then himself, before snuggling into its fleecy folds. Pulling his cap over his eyes he lay thinking and extolling the virtues of sleeping in the open air, unfettered by walls and

Delay in L'Estampe!

roof. He welcomed Mother Nature's gift of silence and perfumes and her many changing faces through the dark night. 'We have a moment to look upon the stars. And there is a special pleasure for some minds in the reflection that we share the same impulse with all outdoor creatures in our neighbourhood; that we have escaped out of the Bastille of civilisation and are become, for the time being, a mere kindly animal and a sheep of Nature's flock.'

Waking during the night, Stevenson had a thirst, which he quenched with clear water from the stream. This rendered him fully awake and he lit a cigarette. Stars shone brightly in the heavens, jewelled patterns that bathed the encircling ribbon of pines with an enchanting glow. There was not a sound save that of Modestine munching the grass contentedly and the ripple of water over stones. A gentle wind floated through the glade as Stevenson thought of the confines of the crowded bedroom of the inn at Chasseradès, of claustrophobic theatres and stifling houses. The outer world appeared a gentler, relaxing place and a source of

Farmers at the Market

infinite pleasure. Although revelling in his solitude, Stevenson felt that something was missing; the companionship of someone to lie beside him. 'For there is a fellowship more quiet even than solitude, and which, rightly understood, is solitude made perfect. And to live out of doors with the woman a man loves is of all lives the most complete and free.'

As Stevenson lay in contemplation he heard a noise drifting from the valley below, which, he discerned, was the sound of a passer-by on the high road, singing with gusto. It would not have seemed so out of place if he had been in a town or city in the dead of night, but nevertheless there was an air of romance about such people who were abroad in the dark hours. Stevenson reasoned that this traveller was fuelled inwardly by drink, but felt that he was quite entitled to engage in song. In this forgiving state of mind he drifted into slumber.

CHAPTER SEVEN

THE FOOT OF MONT LOZÈRE TO THE VALLEY OF THE TARN

When Stevenson awoke once more only the brightest stars were visible and in the east the sun was about to make its entrance. A new day was beginning and he intended to make full use of it. Pulling on his boots and gaiters he broke up some bread, which he fed to Modestine, before gathering water from the stream in his can. This he placed on the spirit lamp and heated some chocolate. Whilst waiting for his drink to boil he watched a streak of vivid orange suffuse the eastern sky and chase away the shadows of the night. He found this wondrous sight exhilarating and became impatient to begin the day's journey.

The hot chocolate drink began to warm him, for a chill wind was blowing and he could see the trees swaying to and fro at its bidding. Hurriedly, he re-packed Modestine's load and before leaving his enchanting hideaway, Stevenson, on impulse, left some coins scattered on the velvet turf, by way of thanks for its pleasing accommodation. He hoped that some needy peasant would find them.

Stevenson continued his lengthy ascent of the Lozère flanks until the path he had followed the previous evening disappeared and he was obliged to follow a line of marker stones, similar to those that had guided him over the Goulet.

The sun was beginning to cast its warmth on the upper reaches of the Lozère and Stevenson removed his jacket, for progress was demanding. However, Modestine took on a new lease of life and, for the first time in his recollection, began to outstrip him. When he stopped for a retrospective view over upper Gévaudan the landscape was tinted azure and gold by the sun's sparkling rays. A number of birds, their curiosity aroused, flew around him or perched on the stone pillars as if standing sentinel.

Almost from the outset of his day's journey Stevenson had detected a faint hissing sound, like that of a steaming kettle. He imagined it could be a waterfall, but none had materialised. As he climbed, the noise increased gradually until breaths of cool air rolled down from the summit. Realisation dawned that the noise was that of a stiff southerly wind raking the slopes on the far side of the mountain and he was close to its crest.

He was soon rewarded by the arrival of the Pic de Finiels, the apex of the mountain. It was akin to entering another world as Stevenson gazed from his lofty perch across a sea of blue hills to the south, stretching as far as the Mediterranean Sea. People tell of spying ships sailing by Montpelier and Sète, from the vantage-point, but no such vessels could be detected in the distant haze. Before him lay southern Languedoc, picturesque, intriguing and romantic; the country of the Camisards.

Around one hundred and eighty years before Stevenson's journey, the Camisards had an encampment on the very spot on which he was standing. It was a land of persecution and reprisal. In 1685 King Louis XIV revoked the Edict of Nantes, which granted religious tolerance to his Protestant subjects, and launched his domain into anarchy and revolt. His action denied the Protestants the right to practice their religion and many fled the country. However, those of the Cévennes, the Camisards, or Cévenoles, opposed the revocation and remained in their mountainous outpost.

In order to force the local people into the Catholic faith, the 'dragonnade,' (detachments of dragoons) were posted to the villages and fed at the expense of the residents. The Cévenoles resisted the dragoons and their opposition finally flared into open revolt. Following the slaying of a Catholic Archbishop in 1702, civil war raged in the Cévennes for two years and carried on to a lesser degree until 1789 when freedom of worship was granted.

Stevenson found that the Camisard uprising had left a lasting impression on the area and its people, which was still much in evidence. The scanty population and the tiny walled settlements he had encountered were a living legacy of the conflict. He had been told by the priest at Our Lady of the Snows that Protestantism remained strong in this seat of the Camisard rebellion where the terror of the Camisards had even forced the Catholic peasants into a revolt of their own. Stevenson had yet to learn if Protestantism was merely

Leaving Coins at the Foot of Mont Lozère

surviving or observed with enthusiasm.

As Stevenson gazed from his elevated viewpoint he saw that those reliable guides, the stone pillars came to a sudden end, but below them was a path that careered down the mountainside, twisting and turning on its precipitous course before plunging into the valley beneath.

Stevenson remembered little of his precarious descent, which was accomplished at a fair speed, other than stopping briefly to allow Modestine to cool her hooves in a stream that crossed their path. Eventually he reached an engaging valley where the track became an undulating road. He could feel the extreme heat in the sheltered defile as he passed many seemingly deserted cabins and he detected no sign of life in the tiny settlements until he was hailed by an urchin, sitting in a nearby meadow.

It was the Sabbath, which probably accounted for the stillness and lack of people. As there was little sign of life Stevenson felt extremely tempted to remove his hot dusty clothes and bathe in the cool waters of the burgeoning River

View From the Summit of Mont Lozère

Rieumalet that flowed by his side. Eventually, his watery companion disappeared into the River Tarn at Le Pont de Montvert. The River Tarn rises in the unforgiving landscape of Mont Lozère and tumbles down to Le Pont de Montvert, the first settlement on its course. He had entered a place of infamous memory, a seat of discontented Protestantism, in which began the Camisard insurrection with the murder of Archbishop Sharp.

Pont de Montvert, an old town with houses clinging to the riverbank, steep alleyways and streets, had an indescribable air of the south and, in contrast to its approach, the town was a hive of activity. At the inn where he had an early lunch, Stevenson was joined by nearly twenty people and later many more entered the hostelry. By crossing the Lozère, he had not only found a different kind of landscape, but the people were also dissimilar. His lunch companions displayed a higher degree of intelligence than Stevenson had previously encountered, with the exception of the railway surveyors at Chasseradès. The good people of

Pont de Montvert were not only interesting and lively, they entertained him with a sword-play of their knives as they ate their meal. All seemed fascinated by Stevenson's journey and one person admitted that if he had the money he would like to emulate him.

Stevenson had not seen a handsome woman since leaving Monastier and this was remedied at lunch, for there were three; two at his table and another waiting on him. The two ladies seated near Stevenson were married, but the serving girl, silent and respectful, gained his approval and it seemed a pity to him that such an attractive young woman should be admired by her country neighbours only. Her beauty should at least be displayed for all to see, he reckoned. As he left the inn Stevenson told the girl of his admiration, but she merely looked steadily at him without embarrassment or emotion.

Pont de Montvert is steeped in the story of the Camisards. As previously mentioned it was here that the conflict broke out, giving rise to an infamous period of persecution and bloodshed. The Protestants were beside themselves with religious zeal and bitterness. It was alleged that in one town all the women seemed possessed by the Devil, suffered trembling fits and uttered prophecies in public. A prophetess of Vivarais was hanged at Montpelier because blood issued from her eyes and nose and she declared she was weeping tears of blood for the oppression of the Protestants. Not only the women were affected. Dependable countrymen, used to tilling the earth, were also seized by convulsions and delivered prophecies as they wailed and lamented. All these sorry acts were the result of twenty years of violent persecution by the dragoons, who left a trail of hanging, burning and torture across the countryside. Men were reduced to rowing in the galleys and women rotted in prisons, but still the flame of Protestantism burned brightly in the Cévennes.

At the forefront of the persecution was Francois de Langlade du Chayla, Archpriest and Inspector of Missions of the Cévennes, who resided periodically in the town of Pont de Montvert. He was thorough, but piratical in nature and at fifty-five had exchanged moderation for a burning anti-religious zeal. Whilst a missionary in China in his youth he was martyred and left for dead. Such misfortune turned du Chayla from a Christian martyr into a Christian persecutor and the Work of the Propagation of the Faith was brutally enforced by him. His dwelling in Pont de Montvert acted as a prison, where he closed the hands of his prisoners onto live coals and plucked out the hair of their beards to make them renounce Protestantism.

Life for the Protestants of the Cévennes became intolerable and escape was strictly forbidden. Despite this edict, a mule driver, familiar with the labyrinth of mountain tracks in the region led several groups of escapées to the safety of Geneva. However, one such convoy was set upon by du Chayla and his supporters. The following Sunday a clandestine meeting of Protestants was held in the woods of Mont Bougès and they were addressed by a wool-carder by the name of Séguier – 'Spirit Séguier' as his associates called him. He insisted that the time had come to act against their repression and they must take up arms to protect their brethren and rid themselves of the Catholic priests.

The following night, of July 24th 1702, a group of fifty strong marched to du Chayla's house at around 10pm singing psalms to announce their presence. The archpriest, alarmed by the prospect of a religious meeting outside his very house ordered his bodyguards to open fire on the Protestants, killing one of their number. The man's enraged comrades battered down the door, overran the ground floor of the prison house and released the prisoners. Courageously, du Chayla's men halted repeated attempts by the Protestants to attain the upper floors of the house, until Séguier gave the order to burn the premises. The fire took hold quickly and the defenders were forced to lower themselves into the garden from upstairs windows, using knotted sheets, and attempt to escape across the river. Du Chayla fell during his attempt and broke his thigh. He was captured and dragged to the centre of the town where, each in turn, Séguier and his Camisards stabbed him, crying as they did so, 'This is for my father broken on the wheel!' 'This is for my brother in the galley!' 'This is for my mother and sisters who were languishing in your evil

Wolves in the Forest

prison!' When it was over the Camisards, who, it is said gained the name during their night's work, knelt to pray and sing psalms around the body of du Chayla until daybreak. Then they marched towards Frugères, a nearby village, to continue their vengeance, leaving the smouldering remnants of du Chayla's house and his multi-pierced body.

Séguier brought about more killings, including a whole family and its servants, but in a matter of days he was captured by the 'dragonnade' and brought to trial. Asked by the judges why he was called 'Spirit,' he answered, 'Because the spirit of the Lord is with me.' When asked where he dwelt, he replied, 'Lately in the desert, soon in heaven.' Found guilty, his right hand was cut off, before he was burned alive.

Stevenson noted in his journal that du Chayla's house had been rebuilt and that the inquisitive could see the terrace-garden into which the archpriest dropped.

On his departure from Le Pont de Montvert Stevenson took to the new road linking it to Florac that lies roughly

Le Pont de Montvert

eight miles to the west. The highway ran along a sandy ledge
perched high on the steep flanks of the gorge through which
threads the lively River Tarn. He found it similar to walking
through the steeply-angled Pass of Killiecrankie, in his native
country, where the Jacobites, led by Viscount 'Bonnie
Dundee' ambushed and routed William III's English troops,
commanded by General Mackay, in 1689. The noise of the
rushing water below and the vista of craggy pinnacles above
added to the landscape's charm, as did the array of Spanish
chestnut trees coating much of the valley. The trees issued a
delicate perfume that tantalised Stevenson's nostrils and the
glorious autumn tints of the vegetation completed an idyllic
scene that he was moved to sketch. Unfortunately, try as he
might he failed to recreate the sun's rays that played upon
and permeated the foliage, which caused him to give up in
anguish.

At that time, the chestnuts mounted on the terraced
hillsides had few people to care for them. The trees were in
a poor state as there were few hands to trim them to foster

correct growth and top nut production. This situation was serious, as the chestnuts were an important source of supply. They provided a staple diet, eaten in soups and stews and they were also diced and ground into flour. The leaves of the trees were fed to livestock, the inner bark was used for basket-making and furniture was produced from the wood.

Stevenson's progress was slow on that balmy afternoon, which was not aided by Modestine's lethargy and the brilliance of his surroundings. As the sun began to descend behind the mountain tops it thrust the valley into shadow and Stevenson began to search for a place to camp for the night. It was a difficult task, due to the narrow terraces and the precipitous nature of the valley sides into which they intruded. He began to worry that if he tried to sleep on a ledge he would wake towards morning to find himself lying in the river below.

At last he found a convenient site; a ledge around sixty feet above the valley floor, large enough for him to spread his sleeping sack on and with a convenient fallen tree forming a parapet to prevent his tumbling down the abrupt slope.

There was no room for Modestine on the narrow shelf and Stevenson had to climb upwards until he found a spot for her to spend the night. It was merely a bed of stones on an artificial ledge, no more than five feet square. He tied the donkey to a convenient chestnut tree and gave her some bread and corn followed by chestnut leaves.

Stevenson's sleeping-place was quite exposed and several carts passed beneath him along the road. As darkness had not yet fallen he tried to hide from their view behind the rampart of the fallen tree. He felt like a hunted Camisard and was fearful of discovery and a visit by inquisitive passers-by during the night.

The air was sultry and his camp was far removed from that of the previous night when he had been safely hidden among the pines of a cool and silent wood. Stevenson realised that he must rise early the when morning came, for signs of labour were all around. Peasants had left many branches, cut from the chestnuts, strewn on the surrounding slope and heaps of leaves were piled against tree trunks awaiting removal for use as fodder for their animals.

When the sun went down, the frogs by the river began their shrill chorus and the night seemed alive with rustling and chirping. An army of ants began to swarm around his resting-place, bats and mosquitoes flew overhead to add to his discomfort. Sleep did not come easily and Stevenson's slumber was disturbed by a scratching sound, coming from beneath his knapsack that served as a pillow. Searching beneath it nothing could be found, but he discovered later that the chestnut plantation was infested with rats that were the probable culprits.

CHAPTER EIGHT

THE VALLEY OF THE TARN TO THE VALLEY OF THE MIMENTE

In the half-light of the following morning he was roused from his sleep by the sound of passing feet that belonged to a peasant who was using a narrow footpath through the trees, undiscovered by Stevenson. The man did not look about him, but disappeared after a few strides into surrounding foliage. It was obviously time for Stevenson to be on the move and he began hurriedly to give Modestine her breakfast as a man and a boy approached. They hailed him and Stevenson waved back, before the pair, who resembled father and son came right up to him. Saying not a word they stood looking at his sleeping sack that lay open with his revolver visible and then transferred their gaze to him. The man broke the long silence. 'You have slept here?' he demanded. Stevenson answered that he had. 'Why?' asked the man. 'I was tired,' replied Stevenson. The questions continued. 'Where are you going and what had you for supper?' When the man's curiosity had been assuaged he said, 'C'est bien' and without explanation he signalled to his son to follow him and they moved to a nearby chestnut tree, which they commenced to prune. Stevenson sighed with relief as the incident had apparently passed off without anger on the man's part. His grave manner and respectability possibly hid a kind and concerned nature.

Recommencing his journey, Stevenson nibbled a cake of chocolate, which served as a makeshift breakfast. As he walked his thoughts returned to the previous night's primitive lodgings, where he had slept fitfully, with ants sharing his sack and disconcerting noises as accompaniment. However, his spirits were raised by his surroundings that looked most attractive on that fine morning. The road soon began to descend to the river and Stevenson took the opportunity to wash in its cool clear waters.

Feeling much revived he carried on his way with a lighter

heart and sang psalms as he progressed. Suddenly, an old woman appeared and without ceremony she demanded money. Here comes the waiter, thought Stevenson, with the bill for his night's lodgings and he handed over some coins without argument. Strangely, this was the only time he was accosted by a beggar during his trek.

A little farther on he was overtaken by a weather-beaten old man, accompanied by a girl, driving two sheep and a goat. The girl walked behind as Stevenson and the man conversed. Eventually the talk turned to religion and the old man enquired if he knew the Lord. When Stevenson replied that they were the best of acquaintances, the kindly man was delighted and, striking his chest said, 'It makes me very happy.' It transpired that there were few in the valley that knew the Lord, 'Many are called,' he declared, 'but few are chosen.' Stevenson implied that it was difficult to really tell who knew the Lord, for those of every faith and even those who worship stones, may know Him and be known by Him. This seemed to please the old man who said that he was in complete agreement with Stevenson's observation. 'We are very few,' he said, 'and are known as Moravians, but in the Department of Gard there are several more, who are called Derbists, after an English pastor.'

Their theological discussion continued until they arrived at the tiny humble settlement of La Vernède, where the man and the girl lived. There were no more than ten dwellings, which were overlooked by a Protestant chapel perched on a hill. After farewells were exchanged Stevenson entered the inn and ordered breakfast. His hosts were an amiable man and his handsome sister. Whilst Stevenson was enjoying breakfast, the village schoolmaster, who had learned of his arrival, called in to talk with him. The teacher declared that all the inhabitants of the village were Protestants, a situation that Stevenson found more pleasing than he would have imagined. What also pleased him was the friendliness of these simple, yet steadfast people, particularly the old man with whom he had walked to the village. This friendly soul had come to the inn to ensure that Stevenson was being cared for and he inquired three times if Stevenson was happy with his meal. The old man did not wish to intrude,

A Happy Couple!

but he seemed so desirous of Stevenson's company that he was touched by his presence, despite the fact that the old man shook his hand at every opportunity.

When the other occupants of the inn had departed to begin their day's work, Stevenson sat for a while talking with the landlord's sister, a girl with a sweet nature and, despite her simple country ways, an engaging sensitivity. She talked at length of the chestnut harvest, the pleasing attributes of the River Tarn and her affection for her family.

The gorge below La Vernède was dramatic as Stevenson continued his journey. Steep crumbling cliffs towered initially on either side, followed by a relenting of the constriction into a greener and wider landscape. He found his progress extremely exhilarating, especially when he came upon the ancient castle of Miral and an embattled monastery. As he passed the black-roofed village of Cocurès, nestling amidst a tapestry of meadows and vineyards, he saw orchards heavy with apples and walnuts being harvested from roadside trees. The hills above the wide valley still thrust skywards, their tops gnarled and aloof and the area appeared benevolent and plentiful. Despite the warmth, the chestnuts had already been gathered and the gold of the trees foretold the advent of winter.

Something in the untamed countryside demonstrated to Stevenson the psyche of the Camisards, who retained a positive and bright outlook, despite their history of bloodshed and violence. Séguier was not forgotten and the people were adamant that God was with them. This, Stevenson thought, was in direct contrast to his native Scots who had fled from the glens to the hills and, despite being certain of the cause for which they fought, harboured foreboding visions and did not share the belief of the Camisards. The people that he encountered in that section of the valley of the Tarn bore their legacy bravely and with admirable patience.

Stevenson soon reached the attractive settlement of Florac standing on the River Tarnon, a branch of the River Tarn, and the seat of the sub-prefecture. The town boasted an ancient castle, an alleyway of plane trees and a fountain

A Farmhouse in the Valley of the Mimente

issuing from a hillside. Known for its handsome women it was one of two capitals of the country of the Camisards.

After a meal in the inn, the landlord took him to a nearby café where Stevenson became the topic of conversation, its customers proving eager for an account of his journey. Surprisingly, he found Catholics and Protestants mixing in a relaxed and amenable manner and also the people shared vivid memories of the religious conflict. They were proud of their ancestors, the Camisards, in the sense that after the subject of his expedition had been exhausted, the conflict became their favourite topic. The hill-folk of the area had evidently not forgotten the era of persecution and tended the graves of local martyrs with respect and care, unlike the so called upper classes of the towns and cities.

Later that afternoon Stevenson received a visit from a Protestant pastor; a well-mannered, likeable young man. They spent an hour or two in conversation, mainly concerning religion and politics. Florac, as Stevenson learned, was part Protestant and part Catholic and the pastor

Camp in the Valley of the Mimente

confirmed that despite the murdering and terror of the past they lived together in relative peace and harmony.

Stevenson sang the praises of the beautiful Tarn Gorge that he had followed from Pont de Montvert, to which the pastor replied, 'It is truly wonderful, but there is even more to the gorge than you have experienced. From Florac the young river Tarn continues through its wild and beautiful valley to Ste-Enimie. The village lies in a sparkling setting beside a bend in the river as it races between the soaring mountainsides of the Causse de Méjean and the Causse de Sauveterre. It is situated on both banks of the Tarn, linked by a medieval bridge. In the larger, northern section the old alleys form a delightful warren. Its twelfth-century church contains some excellent medieval statues. The heart of the village is the lovely Place de Beurre, a delightful, ancient square. Here one can find the old corn market. Above the Place de Beurre is the Place de Plot, a large square in front of the old monastery, gutted by fire at the time of the French Revolution and now partially restored.'

Time was passing and Stevenson declared that he must be on his way once more. He thanked the pastor for his company and conversation, to which the man replied that Stevenson had been a most welcome visitor to his parish. It was a tired donkey and a tired donkey-driver that left Florac in the late afternoon. Stevenson's plan was to follow the Tarnon for a short distance, before entering the valley of the Mimente.

When he crossed a covered wooden bridge over the Tarnon he encountered the valley of the Mimente and it proved equally spectacular to the valley of the Tarn. As Stevenson completed the remaining miles of his day's journey a reddish hue coated the mountains on each side, much of their steep slopes carpeted with chestnut and oak. In the lower reaches the valley was studded with fields of millet, turned scarlet in the evening glow. Trees bearing rosy apples were sprinkled around the valley bottom, tempting to the hungry traveller. However, Stevenson had other priorities, the most pressing being somewhere to lay his head for the night. He passed two tiny villages, offering no places of refuge. Among the oaks and chestnuts the abrupt valley sides offered few opportunities for encampment, being liberally overlaid with a carpet of loose stones, except for patches smothered in heather. As he appraised his surroundings, herdsmen's horns could be heard in the evening stillness, calling flocks to their resting-place. At last Stevenson found a suitable meadow near an angle in the road. He hurried to it and, tethering Modestine to a convenient tree, he scouted around the site as darkness began to close in. Suddenly, he heard children's voices and he discovered a house around the bend in the road and on the opposite bank of the river. Stevenson considered abandoning his campsite, but felt reluctant to do so at nightfall. He determined to make no sound and be on his way in the early morning.

A depression beneath a sturdy oak provided a convenient spot to lay out his sleeping sack. A short trip to the river acquired water that he put on the stove to boil before feeding Modestine. He then ate hungrily in the dark, refraining from lighting his lantern, being so close to the house. Despite the moon lighting the upper slopes of the valley its rays did not penetrate the depths. As Stevenson lay awaiting sleep he gazed at the stars patterning the sky and wondered how many other kindred souls were similarly employed. A powerful wind had risen and it proceeded to scour the valley all night, causing acorns to rain from the bows above him. Despite the wind and it being the first of October, the night was warm and it was not necessary to curl up in his sleeping sack to keep out the cold. The main disturbance was the barking of a dog, an animal that Stevenson feared more than a wolf, which is the more cowardly of the two. He had high regard for dogs in a domestic setting, but on the road or in the countryside he detested them. If attacked, his pistol would have been seen as an offensive weapon Were he to kill a wolf it would be taken as an act of bravery or removing vermin, whereas the killing of a dog could have much worse repercussions. Consequently, Stevenson was greatly discomforted by the continual barking of the infernal animal.

CHAPTER NINE

THE VALLEY OF THE MIMENTE TO ST. GERMAIN DE CALBERTE

Wakened next morning by the barking of the same dog, Stevenson was dismayed to find it charging down the bank towards him. Fortunately, it retreated when he sat up and yelled at it. Further sleep was inadvisable so he fed Modestine and began preparing breakfast. Stars were still visible in a grey-blue sky, typical of early morning. The wind had changed direction and was no longer racing through the valley, but it propelled a voluminous white cloud, tinged with gold by the rising sun, through the heavens.

The elements provided a source of enjoyment as he ate breakfast and his subsequent preparations were soon completed, for he was anxious to be back on the road once more. The lure of journey's end was becoming stronger as he prepared to meet what his penultimate day would bring.

It transpired that his morning was lonely, for he met but one person, who carried a game-bag on his belt. The man made no shame of the fact that he was a Catholic, typifying country people, who retain their own view of the world and are not easily swayed by doctrine and dogma. Stevenson smiled at the thought of Bavile and his dragoons riding brutally over members of a different religious persuasion, but leaving them more determined and vigorous. He could appreciate that rustic people may have little learning, but they do not easily wilt under persecution and their long days of toil give them an affinity with the land and their God. With these thoughts in mind, he passed an enjoyable time conversing with the stout-hearted peasant, who showed a keen interest in Stevenson's expedition and indicated that he was drawing near to his home village of Cassagnas.

After bidding the devout man goodbye, Stevenson approached the remote settlement along a road only recently completed. Its occupants had barely recovered from the arrival of the first cart by that route. Cassagnas comprised a cluster of black roofs on a hillside, among chestnut gardens and overlooked by rocky peaks. The village figured highly in the history of the Camisards, for one of their five arsenals was situated in nearby caves. Here, they stored clothes, corn and weapons, forged bayonets and made gunpowder. The sick and wounded were brought here to recover and were visited by two surgeons and nursed secretly by the women of the neighbourhood. Remarkably, the Camisards of Cassagnas slept without sentries, believing that they were protected by the angels of the God for whom they fought. They belonged to the band of 'Spirit Séguier' and had joined in the singing of the sixty-eighth psalm as they marched with him to the house of du Chayla that unforgettable night

When Louis XVI ended a century of bloodshed and persecution by granting religious tolerance, the people of Cassagnas remained stout Protestants. That is, except for one family, which was of neither religion. It was that of a Catholic priest in revolt who had taken to his bosom a schoolmistress, an act much frowned upon by the villagers!

Stevenson was well received by the plain, but dignified villagers when they learned that he was a Protestant and his knowledge of history earned him further respect. He dined with a gendarme and a merchant who were both Catholics. They were strangers to the village and were pleased to learn of his travels, as were the young men of the house that clustered around them. The men proved very supportive to him and the discussion was amicable, which surprised Stevenson, who was well acquainted with the petty differences of his home country. Upon hearing of Stevenson's nights beneath the stars the merchant became quite agitated, declaring it dangerous to sleep outdoors. He warned of wolves and possible attackers who knew of the Englishmens' reputation for deep purses. However, he recovered sufficiently to ask for one of Stevenson's introductory cards, thinking it would make a good topic of conversation.

In the early afternoon Stevenson crossed the Mimente and took a rugged path up a hillside covered with the indigenous loose stones and heather. At the top the path disappeared, which seemed a common failing of the

Secret Meeting of Protestants

Cévennes. The view from the ridge was breathtaking. To the rear all the rivers flowed to the western ocean and in front lay the Rhone basin. As was the case from the summit of the Lozère, the Gulf of Lyons was clearly visible in good weather. The ridge on which Stevenson was standing formed the heart of Camisard country as four of the five legions camped around it, almost within sight. When Julien had completed his burning and wrecking of the High Cévennes, in 1703, the view from Stevenson's vantage-point would have overlooked an unearthly quiet and de-populated region. Despite the rebuilding and time's healing hand, he found it possibly the wildest view of his whole journey. Row upon row of peaks, carved by millions of years of erosion, thrust southwards, the intervening valleys deep in shadow.

As Stevenson searched for a downward path an extremely aged shepherd approached leaning heavily on a pair of sticks. How has such an old man arrived here, wondered Stevenson? Yet more intriguing was the question as to how he would escape from this lofty ridge. Having the decency to refrain from these questions, he asked the man for guidance. The shepherd was well acquainted with the hills

Locomotive in the Valley of the Mimente

and pointed the way to the road heading for St. Germain de Calberte. Stevenson thanked him for his assistance and had begun to make his descent when the old man called to him. Turning round, Stevenson saw him beckoning with one of his sticks, so, leaving Modestine he returned to the ridge to find that the shepherd wished to know what wares he was selling. The man was under the impression that he was a pedlar! 'Nothing,' replied Stevenson, bristling. 'Nothing at all?' queried the old man. 'Absolutely nothing!' said Stevenson, turning on his heel and leaving the nonplussed shepherd scratching his head in bewilderment.

Stevenson descended with Modestine to the road, which snaked through an avenue of chestnuts. Despite the presence of several hamlets and the remote houses of chestnut farmers in the valley it was a solitary march that afternoon. Evening came early and the voice of a woman could be heard at dusk crooning a sad, interminable ballad that appeared to concern love and sweethearts. 'Ah!' Stevenson murmured, 'love that makes the world go round, but can bring sweethearts close only to separate them once more. Hope is the only true emotion that wipes away the tears of life and endures for a lifetime.'

At nightfall the road that they were following joined a broader and dustier highway. The moon shone brightly in the heavens, casting long shadows in the gloom and Stevenson was moved to take a bottle of wine from his belongings, having discarded the remains of his unsavoury brandy, and drink to their light-giving companion. Invigorated, he quickened his step and even Modestine seemed rejuvenated, as she offered no resistance.

They followed the winding road at a good pace as it continued to descend amongst masses of chestnuts. An amenable warm breeze fanned them from time to time, but the night was otherwise still and silent. Dust flew from beneath their feet and their shadows hurried before them, as though eager to end their march. When they turned one of the many bends in the writhing road, St. Germain de Calberte appeared without warning, raising Stevenson's spirits even further. However, all was in darkness save the light from an open door. Two women stood nearby chattering, despite the late hour, and seemed shocked at the sudden appearance of a man leading a donkey. They did, however, direct Stevenson to the inn, where he was not very well received. The landlady was busily engaged in putting her children to bed, which she had to curtail in order to rejuvenate the dying embers of the fire. This was carried out with reluctance and much grumbling. A little later Stevenson retired to bed without supper.

CHAPTER TEN

ST. GERMAIN DE CALBERTE TO ST. JEAN DU GARD

Next morning Stevenson was awakened by a multitude of cocks crowing their hearts out. Creeping to the window of his comfortable room he looked out on a lovely sun-drenched morning and a host of chestnut gardens. Eager to be abroad he dressed hurriedly and went to explore his surroundings.

Despite it being the capital of a canton, he found St. Germain de Calberte barely larger than a hamlet. It lay terraced across a steep slope in the midst of great chestnuts. Its parish measured eighteen miles in circumference and the village was much larger at one time, comprising 275 households. It was decimated during the years of bloodshed and retribution when its inhabitants were reduced to a mere handful. Du Chayla kept a library here and also held a court of missionaries. Intending this to be his last resting-place he had a tomb erected, with a view to lying among the grateful villagers, who he had redeemed from delusion. The day after he was killed his body was brought here, scarred with its many wounds, and it was laid out in state in the church. A rousing sermon was preached by the Parish priest, who urged his brethren to give their lives for the cause, as their murdered archpriest had done. The service was rudely interrupted by news of 'Spirit Séguier's' proximity and the whole congregation scattered and fled, accompanied by the priest, who did not stop until he reached the safety of Alais!

This tiny enclave of Catholicism was an oasis in a desert of Protestantism, surrounded as it was by the Camisard legions. The priest who had fled from du Chayla's funeral service, kept the faith, returned to St. Germain de Calberte and denounced continually the wrong-doings of the Protestants. Saloman, a leader of one of the nearby Camisard legions, besieged the village for over an hour, but his forces were eventually beaten back. The dragoons guarding the priest and his church were heard, whilst the battle was raging, singing Protestant psalms and consorting

Le Pont du Gard

with the attackers. The following morning it was discovered they had handed over their powder to the Camisards in exchange for money. So much for guaranteeing the safety of the priest they were guarding!

On Stevenson's tour of the village that fine morning, all was so quiet and peaceful it seemed as though the earlier conflict was but a dream. He found the Protestant chapel standing on a ledge below the village and its counterpart, the ancient Catholic Church in the centre of the village. Everywhere he went Stevenson was scrutinised by the inquisitive inhabitants and followed, at a distance, by their equally curious children.

In order to escape all the attention, he took to the terraces and began to sketch the chestnut trees and their leafy canopies. His surroundings were green and restful and Stevenson felt a quiet contentment, rarely having enjoyed a place so much.

He dined at lunch with a Catholic couple who agreed with the condemnation of a Catholic young man who had

Bargaining for Modestine

married a Protestant girl and joined her religion. 'It is wrong for a man to change,' they declared, as they drank La Parisienne over lunch, made from the watered down juice of the local grape. It was a weak drink, but very tasty and a considerable amount was consumed during their long discussion. Mid afternoon had arrived before they said their farewells and Stevenson departed St. Germain de Calberte.

He and Modestine descended beside the Gardon of Mialet, a great dried up watercourse. He progressed through St. Etienne Vallée Française and towards evening made a long, steep ascent of the hill of St. Pierre. During this climb he was followed, and eventually overtaken by an empty carriage, whose driver also thought he was a pedlar. The man was convinced Stevenson was dealing in blue woollen collars, worn by French draught horses, having noticed the blue wool hanging from either end of his pack.

Urging Modestine onwards, he was anxious to enjoy the view over the hill before nightfall. Unfortunately, it was dark when he reached the summit. In the moonlight the outline of distant hills could be seen, but the yawning valley beneath was engulfed in darkness. Stark against the sky was Mount Aigoual that had been the bastion of another Camisard leader, Castanet, whose reputation as an energetic leader was matched by his loyalty to his wife. In the midst of the conflict he married a beautiful girl named Mariette, amidst great rejoicing. To mark the splendid match, Castanet released twenty-five Catholic prisoners. Some months later, Mariette was arrested by the authorities, much to Castanet's anger and dismay. In reprisal he took a Catholic lady hostage, thereby securing the release of his lovely wife.

Stevenson and Modestine took their last meal together on the summit of St. Pierre, whilst he sat upon a pile of stones and the donkey ate bread from his hand. He had found that Modestine would eat more readily in this manner, for she seemed to have developed a liking for him. Unfortunately, this affection would shortly be betrayed.

Their meal over, the pair began the long descent to St. Jean du Gard and maintained a good pace. The only person they encountered on the final leg of their journey together was a carter with moonlight glinting on his lantern and lighting up his features. Such was their progress that Stevenson was eating supper at the inn in St. Jean du Gard before 10pm, happy in the knowledge that they had covered fifteen miles and scaled demanding St. Pierre in just over six hours.

Stevenson enjoyed a restful night's sleep knowing that his testing, but engrossing and enlightening journey lay behind him. There would be no need to rise early on the morrow.

After an agreeable breakfast Stevenson went to the inn's stable in search of Modestine. He was disturbed to see her lack-lustre appearance and approached the ostler, who was feeding a nearby horse. It transpired that the man had already fed and examined the donkey and he announced that she was unfit to travel for at least two days. Eager to reach Alais to collect his mail, Stevenson cold-heartedly decided to abandon Modestine and take a stagecoach.

As she had achieved a good pace in the latter stages of

Performing Animals

their journey Stevenson thought Modestine would make a fair bargain for another owner. He gave word to the occupants of the inn and to some townspeople that she was for sale, adding that it was a golden opportunity for her purchaser. Several derisory offers were forthcoming during the morning and, desperate to make a sale, Stevenson found a buyer willing to pay thirty-five francs for the donkey, complete with saddle. This was below the expected price, but he needed a swift transaction.

Stevenson found St. Jean du Gard an extensive place; a

typical Cévenole settlement and largely Protestant. It boasted an ancient bridge over one of the numerous Gardons, which unite to form the Gard. During his examination of the district Stevenson noticed that the surrounding vineyards had been ravaged by phylloxera, a common louse. It explained why he had been obliged to drink La Parisienne in St. Germain de Calberte.

A little later he came across a group of men by the river using a cider press and one of the party confirmed that they were reduced to making cider, adding vehemently that the country was in a dire state.

During his stay at the inn, Stevenson was approached by the Protestant mayor, who craved his assistance. Many young women of the Cévennes sought employment in England as a governess, due to the common religion and difference in language. Could Stevenson help one such woman who had received circulars from two different agencies in London and was unsure how to respond? Stevenson agreed to help and gave what assistance he could.

After lunch he boarded the stage for Alais and it was not until it departed that he suddenly realised that he and Modestine would not meet again. Despite his animosity towards the recalcitrant donkey, he felt lost without her. They had been bosom companions for nearly a fortnight, trudged over 120 miles and combated heat, thirst and exhaustion. Towering rocky ridges had been scaled and many a lonely road traversed. Despite her unyielding interludes and frequent slow pace, she had been a faithful companion that eventually began to worship him, hence her eagerness to eat from his hand. She had borne the excessive load and the chafing of its straps with fortitude and patience.

Stevenson hoped she would find a good home and live a contented life. These thoughts brought a lump to his throat and, despite the proximity of the stage driver and four male passengers, he began to weep, just as Father Adam had when he sold her to him.

PART 2

(An account of the author's journey in 2007)

The Author's Route

CHAPTER ONE

LE MONASTIER TO ARLEMPDES

A benevolent sun beamed upon me as I gazed from the old town of Le Monastier over the valley that was to form the first stage of my journey through the Cévennes in the footsteps of Robert Louis Stevenson. As I sat enjoying some refreshment at a conveniently sited picnic table, I pondered on the fact that he would have overlooked the same valley before setting out with Modestine, the reluctant donkey. What he would not have seen were the modern houses, tennis courts and campsite set within it, but the wooded slopes coating the verdant hollow and the view to the distant mountains would be little changed. They glistened in the sunshine, an inviting foretaste of what lay ahead.

Nearby is the plaque denoting the starting-point of Stevenson's journey all those years ago. It declares 'From here, on the 22nd of September 1878, departed Robert Louis Stevenson for his voyage to traverse the Cévennes with a donkey.' A very pleasant starting-point, I reckoned and wondered why he had chosen it. He makes no mention of this in *Travels with a Donkey*, or his reason for undertaking such a journey. As mentioned earlier, he had travelled to the Auvergne some time before his departure and spent roughly a month in Le Monastier. The townsfolk were eager to help with his preparations and before he had taken one step he was lauded, given free meals and his health frequently toasted. I imagine that after all this attention and adulation he had to go through with it!

Following my own arrival in Le Monastier I had toured the town, investigating its narrow streets, constricted by tall, three, four and even five-storey buildings, little altered since Stevenson's time. Red pantiles, shuttered windows, and balconies could be found in abundance, together with many figures of Our Lady (the Virgin) set into walls. Another striking feature was the presence of several fountains. To add a little modernity, the town has general stores, and boulangeries offering enticing crusty breads, rolls, mouthwatering pastries and other confections. One slight problem I experienced was that shops closed at lunchtime for several hours so one had to purchase food, souvenirs, postcards and medical supplies, if required, in the morning. It was Wednesday and several establishments in the town were closed for the day, including the Office de Tourisme and the Museum Municipal. The latter is housed in an impressive chateau that stands proudly in the town's upper reaches.

I passed the Gite D'Etape where Stevenson stayed, which has the dates 1887 and 1993 above the entrance and a small representation of him and Modestine by the doorway. I was less successful in locating the Hotel Morel, now a private house, which was Stevenson's home during his stay in Le Monastier. What a pity there was no blue plaque in evidence.

The older inhabitants of the town appear similar in character to those Stevenson would have known and to prove that some of the old ways still exist, I came across a woman sweeping her yard with a besom.

I had stayed the previous night in Le Puy and reached Le Monastier in the late morning, having brought with me a sizeable picnic lunch provided by the hotel. This I was preparing to eat when a camper van drew up, from which a middle-aged couple emerged and began setting the adjacent picnic table. They put on a tablecloth, a vase of flowers, a bottle of wine and glasses, obviously keen on their home comforts. Meanwhile, I sat munching a baguette, one portion filled with meat, the other with soft cheese; accompanied by a tomato, hard-boiled egg, small tub of syrup and fruit. The hotel had served me well, too well in fact, for I felt reluctant to walk after such a feast. From then onwards I existed on a bottle of water, a pastry and fruit during each day's walk. This was all that was required, particularly on days involving extreme heat and prodigious climbs.

My first day's walk was merely a warm up, according to my notes, covering fourteen and a half kilometres (nine miles). They were to prove somewhat understated in terms of distance and I was to experience some very long sections.

Touching the Stevenson plaque for good luck I left Le

Monastier in brilliant sunshine and descended into the valley to cross the River Gazeille. I spotted the comforting red and white markings of the GR 70 as I made my descent, but noted that they were merely lines painted on trees or rocks. Subsequently, I had to keep a sharp eye out for them for they were apt to be obscured by foliage or worn by the ravages of weather.

The first of several of the day's testing climbs began as I was introduced to the rough, stony tracks that are a prominent feature of the GR 70. Many of these were the main roads of Stevenson's time, trod by packhorse and drover. Views were at a premium as I laboured through verdant Malaval woods, eventually emerging onto a plateau, which afforded fine long-distance views over a rippling landscape of tree-coated hills and distant mountains, fading into a blue haze.

I was now on a broad track that once formed part of the ancient route from Le Monastier to Pradelles, which aroused a feeling of somehow becoming involved in the history of the region. I could imagine ancient travellers, heads bowed against a searching wind and driving rain battling their way, across mountain and valley, ill-shod and poorly-clothed, eking out a living by transporting goods along the rough highways of their time.

My reverie was interrupted by the arrival of the tiny settlement of Le Cluzel, where I passed the first of many stone crosses I would encounter, its setting enhanced by bowers of resplendent red roses.

A little farther on, I came to Courmaces, where I took refuge from the searing sun, on a welcome rustic bench, in the shade of a convenient oak tree. I had been advised to take plenty of liquid on my journey and began to take healthy gulps from my bottle of water, as I was already coated in sweat. The cover afforded by the overhanging branches was, unfortunately, also being enjoyed by a battalion of flies, a species with whom I was to become well acquainted over the succeeding days. In my efforts to repel them I began to wave my arms like a demented loon and an old woman that happened to be passing, shook her head at my antics.

Stevenson Plaque, Le Monastier

During intervals in my arm-thrashing I noticed a small shrine nearby, constructed in stone, bedecked with flowers and containing a figure of Our Lady, that formed what was to become another familiar sight. As if to complement the edifice, a gable-end wall, all that remained of an ancient building, loomed over it. Could it have once been a little place of worship, I wondered?

Seemingly tired of my company, the flies abandoned me and my little spot became idyllic. A soft breeze sprang up, cooling my fevered brow and birds chirped merrily, with French accents (tuite! tuite!), in the surrounding trees

I took to the road once more, a dirt one in this instance, to the village of Le Cros, where I became of great interest to several dogs in the vicinity. A barking chorus rang in my ears and I decided to make a speedy exit. As I did so I was chaperoned from the place by a large dog that I had no desire to offend. Stevenson remarked on his dislike of dogs in the countryside and I was therefore wary of them, but although I encountered many, I was never attacked.

Chateauneuf, near Le Monastier

The next settlement I entered on that hot afternoon was St. Martin de Fugères, basking attractively beneath a cloudless sky. I found the place extremely appealing, apart from the fact that a rebuilding project was in progress right in its centre, with the attendant upheaval and debris. The village has a well-maintained War Memorial, with large shells and an impressive cannon at its base. I found that all such memorials, in addition to the shrines, were exceedingly well-kept, and also bedecked with flowers and other tokens of remembrance. The local stone, with its engaging brown tone, gives the buildings a particular allure. Pride of place must go to its church, fronted by a most impressive façade. Stevenson found it overflowing on the Sabbath, but it stood empty as I surveyed it. I wondered if it would be as full during worship today. Such an imposing building deserved to have many worshippers.

A short time later, as I began to descend a steep rocky track, an exciting vista unfolded beneath me. Deep in the valley below lay Goudet, on a bend in the sparkling Loire.

Its cluster of red roofed dwellings sat amongst emerald-green meadows, a veritable oasis amongst the encircling wooded hills. Stevenson likened it to Shangri-La, a remote haven linked only to the outside world by a series of mountain tracks. The D49 road now threads through it and the tranquil tree-lined river winds beneath the ruins of the Chateau de Beaufort, perched on a rocky pinnacle. I immediately recognised the ruin, from the sketch that Stevenson had made of it. Another striking feature is the craggy volcanic mound that stands guard over the village centre.

Keen to see the place at close quarters, I clambered down the intimidating track as fast as I dare, not wishing to fall headlong and bring my journey to an abrupt end. The village proved just as attractive at ground level and much as Stevenson describes it, as I made for the rather undistinguished bridge spanning the Loire. However, the view from it, along the rocky riverbanks, was adequate compensation as the sun reflected off brilliant-white walls and red pantiles and lit the terraced slopes above. Stevenson used a nearby vantage-point for sketching the chateau, which is much more intact in his view of it. More of its walls have crumbled, but substantial parts still remain.

I ascended the steep road from the village that passes an entrance to the chateau, but the gate was barred and I had to be content with a long-distance photograph of its remains.

The steep climb through woods that followed was tortuous and sweat poured from me. Instead of a donkey to accompany me I could have used a 'punkah wallah' to dispatch the hordes of flies that encircled me. Despite it being the first day of my journey and only several miles covered I was beginning to feel the strain. All I need is a room and a bed, to lay my head, was one of the thoughts that tumbled into my mind, which went into overdrive. It conjured up the view of Julie Andrews singing 'All I want is a room somewhere,' that immortal line from *My Fair Lady*. I had read recently that Julie was nearly dismissed from the show before its Broadway opening, being unable to 'cut it' during rehearsals. Rex Harrison, who was playing Professor Higgins became exasperated by her poor performance. During a Friday rehearsal he declared vehemently, 'If that bitch is here on Monday, I'm through!' Thankfully, the director took drastic action and worked with Julie on her part for the entire weekend and produced the desired improvement.

What a wimp, I thought of myself. Stevenson had not only to contend with these conditions, but also had to drag along a recalcitrant donkey whose load would not remain secure. I paused for a drink from my bottle, (I drank a litre of water that afternoon!) squared my shoulders and pressed on.

After what seemed an age the trees relented and the terrain levelled. I flopped into long grass by the side of the track I was following, in order to record my thoughts on that baking afternoon in the hope that people may find them remotely interesting. Tragically, as I wrote, a legion of flies joined me and buzzed around my head with gay abandon, driving me from my resting-place.

I came to a narrow road, but was immediately directed from it by the now familiar red and white signs onto a path that led me through a dense wood. As I negotiated the narrow thoroughfare I met a team of horse-riders, coming in the opposite direction, on fine steeds. Their mounts looked in first-class condition and they were thankfully well-behaved, passing me with care on the restricted path. For the next mile or so I had to dodge the droppings that they had kindly deposited on my route, performing a kind of jig in the process.

Eventually, I emerged from the trees to be greeted with the uplifting sight of the Hotel Du Manoir, my night's resting-place. It lies in a lovely setting, amongst a huddle of buildings, dominated by another ruined chateau that is set on a massive rock. The River Loire has cut a deep channel between this block of basalt and an even larger escarpment as it winds past the picturesque hamlet. Arlempdes is a place for photographers and the scene I have just described features widely on postcards and magazines. I noticed in the hotel reception that tickets could be obtained there for a tour of the chateau ruins, with a guide in summer. From photographs it appeared that one or two buildings within the

Hotel du Manoir, Arlempdes

ruins were intact, but as my stay was short, I was unable to visit and discover if they were occupied. However, I did discover that the final owner of the chateau was the Laval family, who purchased it in the early eighteenth century and later abandoned it. The last descendant of the family bequeathed it to the Prado's Community of Lyon, in 1936. An association was then formed to preserve what remained of it.

I took the opportunity, in late evening, to investigate the exterior of the church and old manor house that lies beneath the chateau in a cobbled courtyard dominated by a towering, weather-beaten gateway. I gazed upward in awe at the gigantic rock face above me, marvelling at the builders who had the courage and expertise to erect a castle in such an impregnable position.

The hotel looked inviting, with tables arranged on the terrace in front of its attractive mature-stone façade. It was obviously well-run, I discovered as I entered and was immediately requested to remove my walking boots and leave them in the lobby. The establishment was family-run and the lady of the house, who appeared to run the place, was very efficient, to the point of being slightly officious.

Dinner that evening was excellent and the beef bourguignon was delicious. I discovered the French custom of serving cheese between the main course and dessert. I did find this too much at times and although I could have dispensed with dessert, I have a sweet tooth and that would never do!

To add to my pleasure, the view through the expansive dining room window over the tree-studded valley beneath was not to be missed. As I admired my surroundings between courses the tribulations of the afternoon's walk became a distant memory and I was already looking forward to what tomorrow would bring. During the meal I had a brief chat with a couple on the next table, who were touring the area by car. As I explained earlier, my French is not very proficient and I was unable to converse at length with them. However, I detected an Australian accent from the next table but one and after the meal I introduced myself to the couple. They were also walking the Stevenson Trail, known in France as 'Le Chemin de Stevenson.' I discovered that they had also walked extensively in other countries, including England, having completed Wainwright's 190-mile Coast to Coast Walk, from St.Bees, on the Cumbrian coast to Robin Hood's Bay. They were also familiar with the Yorkshire Dales and Lake District. The most demanding walk the man had tackled was in New Guinea, along what is now a recognised trail that follows the route of the Japanese advance through the island during the Second World War. From a map of the region you can see how close the invaders came to reaching Australia. Apparently, the trail must be walked with a guide, and a machette is needed! The friendly couple plan to return to Yorkshire and attempt the Cleveland Way that runs from Helmsley to Saltburn, on the east coast, and down to Filey, where it meets the Wolds Way.

CHAPTER TWO

ARLEMPDES TO PRADELLES

The following morning dawned bright and sunny, which was just as well, as a tough day's walk lay ahead. At breakfast the Australians asked if I had heard the thunderstorm during the night, to which I had been completely oblivious. I must have slept soundly

Breakfast was served by the chef, who was responsible for the splendid dinner the previous evening and, although he spoke a little English we had some difficulty in communicating. As you will be aware, a fried breakfast is not an option in France and as I looked at the croissants and crisply-toasted bread, I felt I needed more to sustain me on the long day's march. 'Avez vous les cereals?' I inquired. The chef looked puzzled. Then I had an idea. 'Kelloggs?' 'Ah, oui!' he replied and hurried to the kitchen. I had difficulty keeping a straight face when he returned with a child's size packet of Coco Pops! I found throughout my journey that 'Kelloggs,' for cereal and 'Heineken,' for beer were universally known.

It was soon time to lace my boots and tackle the thirty two-kilometre (twenty-mile) stage to Pradelles. My route-plan indicated backtracking nearly to Goudet, before striking west to Ussel. Rather than face the forest tracks once more I decided to cut off the corner, as it were and take the winding D54 road on a north-westerly route to the village.

I was soon passing through the hamlet of Freycenet, to which I must admit I paid scant respect, for my mind was set on reaching Ussel as quickly as possible. Having no time to waste, I was in no mood to linger. Extensive road walking can be boring, but the compensation of open countryside and wide vistas made it an option. As I approached Ussel, following a sustained climb from Arlempdes, I rejoined the GR 70 and progressed to a road junction, where the D54 meets the D49 road. The latter led me, in a westerly direction, into the elevated village that boasts several fifteenth and sixteenth-century houses scattered around its centre. The finest of these is the turreted Hotel de Ventadour, which, along with a giant, somewhat battered granite eagle, form the most notable attractions. The eagle stands in Place Voltaire and acts as a reminder of a former Roman settlement that existed nearby.

My passage through Ussel was speedier than that of Stevenson, who had great trouble with Modestine. Her saddle and pack slid over to rest beneath her stomach, requiring a frustrating period spent rectifying the misfortune. However, this was not the end of his tribulations, for, on the move once more, the donkey tried to enter every house and courtyard that they passed. Stevenson's temper was not improved by the mirth of the villagers that observed Modestine's antics.

Bidding farewell to Ussel I took the GR 70 track out of the village and into a valley overlooked by fir-covered mountains, some of which Stevenson referred to as 'sugar-loaves.' Mont Marelle and Pauilles looked down pityingly upon me as I trudged towards the tiny hamlet of Preyssac, nestling beneath a ring of fells. I was still climbing and the slope seemed never-ending. By the time I reached Bouchet St. Nicholas the elevation had reached 1,219 metres (4,000 feet).

Stevenson arrived at Bouchet late in the evening, exhausted, shivering and discouraged after his long day's march from Le Monastier. His difficulties with Modestine had contributed to his wretched state, but his spirits lifted when he came upon an inn that offered sanctuary. Despite the earth floor, the inedible omelette and undrinkable wine he was given, he felt more at ease when he was shown to a room containing two beds. Imagine his chagrin when he discovered that he was to share the room with a young couple and their child, one bed for him and the other for the family, who were just retiring for the night. Feeling embarrassed and uncomfortable, he spent a restless night, despite his desperate tiredness.

The inn has now gone so no longer will you be obliged to share a room with strangers!

Bouchet St. Nicholas is a pleasant place, but is probably smaller today than when Stevenson passed through. Like its

Statue of Stevenson and Modestine, Bouchet St. Nicholas

neighbour, Ussel, it has its share of history. In addition to a striking thirteenth-century castle it contains an ancient house whose stone walls are embellished with bas-reliefs, depicting hunting scenes.

On the outskirts of the village stands a wooden carving of Stevenson and Modestine, mounted on a tall wooden base. Carved on the base is the following inscription:

Le 22 Septembre 1878 R. L. Stevenson et Modestine font étape au Bouchet St. Nicholas. (The 22 September 1878 R. L. Stevenson and Modestine made Bouchet St. Nicholas their stopping-place)

I would like to have visited Lac du Bouchet that Stevenson headed for, but never reached. It is a mere two kilometres from the village, so Stevenson did not miss it by a wide margin. It lies in a volcanic crater formed around 300, 000 years ago and is completely enclosed by pine trees, arranged in regimented rows. The lake is very popular with fishermen as it contains a plentiful supply of fish, of a wide variety.

Unfortunately, time was pressing and the day's journey was far from complete. The GR 70 changes direction as it leaves Bouchet St. Nicholas and heads south-east on a gradual decline. All the energy I had expended in climbing to Bouchet was now being negated, but the going was easier, naturally.

My next destination was the village of Landos, which proved disappointing. Its undistinguished main street leads to the market square, where several three and four-storey buildings add a little appeal. The town hall seemed worthy of inspection but was barred and shuttered, which, in my opinion, summed up the lack-lustre village. I even had a problem in leaving it! The GR 70 had been diverted a short distance from the village and I had trouble following the diversion, which led me well off of my intended route. I spent a frustrating twenty minutes at one point walking back and forth to ensure I was going in the right direction. In the absence of signs I blundered into the hamlet of Praclaux and managed, eventually, to regain the GR 70

It was with great relief that I put this disappointing episode behind me and made for Jagonas, a hamlet lying

Bas-relief, Bouchet St. Nicholas

four kilometres from Landos. This tiny settlement proved far more attractive and I found a picnic table on its small village green. I decided to rest awhile and have some refreshment. It was very hot and I drank deeply from my bottle of water. As I ate, a cat and a cockerel crept up to me, warily and I fed them also. The amiable owner of a house overlooking the green joined me at the table and became very interested in my journey. I explained about following Stevenson, and how he was able to converse at greater length with the people he encountered, having lived in France for a considerable period.

As we talked a white van sped into view, its horn blaring, and stopped by the edge of the green. I began to complain about the noise, but my companion laughed and explained that the driver supplied provisions. In no time several villagers appeared and formed a queue at his van; the man was obviously in great demand.

I was soon on the move once more, continuing south-east. The landscape was one of green meadows, topped by rolling hills, a most pleasant setting. A sign indicated that the hamlet of Arquejols was close at hand and, after passing

82

Arquejols

through the sleepy settlement I followed a narrow, winding road into a deep valley, crossed by a very impressive railway viaduct. It towered above me with a shapely hill forming a stimulating backdrop. The hill is, in fact, an extinct volcano, a reminder that I was passing through the Vélay, a land of ancient volcanic activity and spectacular gigantic cones, such as those in Le Puy.

Road-walking ended as quickly as it had begun, when I was obliged to take a steep path up the flank of La Garde. I met four French ladies at this point, who were walking part of the GR 70 to see how they coped. We chatted for several minutes, for as long as my pigeon French allowed, before I pressed on alone. The climb stiffened and I began to regret my haste. Sweat was pouring from me once again and the strain was considerable. Despite this, I was pleased with my progress and seemed to be coping pretty well with the long day's march. I had found on other long walks that you tend to become fitter as the days go by and I actually felt better than on the previous day.

After several stops for a drink of water I was pleased to see the track begin to descend to a road that links the hamlets of Les Uffernets and Beaune. The views were extensive as the next section of the journey rolled out before me; a green and inviting panorama sprinkled with evergreens. When I crossed the road the track levelled out for roughly a kilometre before climbing once more. Unbeknown to me at the time, it was the final uphill section before the long descent through a forest to Pradelles.

I recalled that Stevenson had little to say about the section of his journey from Bouchet St.Nicholas to Pradelles, apart from it being bleak, bitterly cold and solitary. The only people he met on the road were 'a cavalcade of stride-legged ladies and post-runners.' What he called a road would be today's tracks, accessible on foot, or horseback only.

My pace slowed and the climb tamed me, for the many miles I had travelled that day began to take their toll. Even this turned out more favourable than negotiating the next section of tortuous stony track, descending through a dense forest, with views blotted out. After what seemed an age I emerged from the trees to enjoy a fine view of journey's end for the day. I found Pradelles delightful. Even as I approached, the old town, set prominently on a hill above the valley of River Allier, seemed to offer a splendid welcome. The sun glinted on the roof of its church that towers above the cluster of mellow buildings around it.

As I entered its main street I passed four elderly local inhabitants sitting on a wall. Glad of the respite, I sat beside them to pass the time of day. They were rather amused to discover I was walking the Chemin de Stevenson and declared that they had no wish to do so at their age. 'Where do you live?' one of them inquired. When I replied, 'Yorkshire,' there were signs of recognition from them. I was to find during my journey that many French people were aware of Yorkshire. I did not push my luck by asking if they were familiar with Ilkley Moor. I doubt if they had heard the Yorkshire anthem, *On Ilkley Moor Bah't 'at*!

Pradelles is seemingly untouched by time. Its venerable buildings have character, some extremely so. A stone fountain forms the centre-piece of the main square that is surrounded by neat, white-walled premises. An inviting

View from Le Monastier

Ancient Route from Le Monastier to Pradelles

Goudet

Chateau and Village of Arlempdes

Jagonas – Village Green

Viaduct near Arquejols

Pradelles

Pradelles – Chapelle Notre Dame

River Allier – Langogne

Langogne

Chateau – Luc

Laveyrune – Cycle Race

La Bastide Puylaurent

Abbaye de Notre Dame des Neiges (Our Lady of the Snows)

Courtyard of Notre Dame des Neiges

Dolmen ('The Giant's Palette') – Le Thort

Street in Pradelles

café/bar and a general store occupy one corner of the square, which also houses an impressive War Memorial topped by the statue of a proud soldier dressed in blue. From the square, a warren of narrow cobbled streets leads down to its most prominent buildings, the church and the Chappelle de Notre Dame. As you pass through this labyrinth the mature stone walls and cobbles of the ancient passages give the confines a soft brown hue. At the foot of the town the medieval archway that was once the entrance to the town's precincts, still stands intact near the church.

I was eager to enter the twelfth-century church, with its fifteenth-century facade, particularly to see the wooden figure of Our Lady of Pradelles, so ignored by Stevenson. Its interior was impressive and I soon located the diminutive figure of her, holding a small child. She is colourfully attired, but does not have a commanding presence, which one would expect from someone able to perform miracles. Who am I to say that she could not? It all depends on the strength of one's belief.

It is a short distance to the Chappelle de Notre Dame that was built in 1623 and is topped by a shapely tower overlooking the striking green carpet of meadows that rolls down to the Allier. The chapel contains, naturally, a statue of Our Lady, and was a place of pilgrimage for the region in former times. According to a text of 1672, a curious custom was observed in offering domestic animals as a way of acceptance into the chapel congregation.

In 1612 a convent was established opposite where the chapel stands, home to brothers of the Order of Saint Dominique, and Pradelles became a bastion of Catholicism. This is probably the reason why Stevenson, being a Protestant, declined to enter the chapel, or to see the figure of Our Lady of Pradelles in the church, although requested to by the landlady of the inn where he had lunch

Another relic of Pradelles' rich past is a tablet on the wall of a building tucked away in one of the streets that radiate from Le Place de la Halle. It marks Maison Natale, home to a local heroine, Jean la Verde, commonly called La Verdette. In 1588 she saved the town from plunder during a dawn raid by a Protestant band of marauders, by slaying its leader. She hurled a large stone from the ramparts onto the head of Jacques de Chambert, their captain, which broke up the attack.

I called in the Office de Tourisme (Tourist Office) in search of information concerning the town. To my surprise I came face to face with two of the ladies who I had met earlier in the day, They were in good spirits, having completed their day's walk without too much difficulty and they planned to do more sections of Le Chemin de Stevenson.

Outside the office stands one of the many signboards to be found along the GR 70, advertising the walk. It displayed a picture of the area with a photograph of Stevenson and the monument, 'La Hall aux Grains,' in Langogne, superimposed upon it. Langogne is not far from Pradelles and it lay on my route.

That evening, despite tiredness due to my extensive day's walk, I was feeling good as I sat down to sample what I hoped would be an appetising dinner. The hotel was fairly small, but with several storeys and typical of the older-style 'auberge.' My room was on the top floor and there were several projections in the ceiling, which I had to take care to avoid. Consequently, I moved around with head and shoulders bent like Quasimodo, which rekindled memories of walking Offa's Dyke Path some years previously when I spent a night in a similar top-storey garret in the market town of Kington.

The dining room was nearly full and people were being served by a speedy lone waiter who had ten tables to accommodate. He flitted between kitchen and dining room and around the tables like Rudolph Nureyev, which caused me to marvel at his adroitness. When he approached my table I inquired if he spoke English, which appeared to throw a spanner in the works, for he retreated rapidly. I was obviously trouble and could upset his whirlwind routine. He returned some time later and deposited a menu and a bottle of water on the table before hastily withdrawing once more. How was I going to cope with the language and this darting waiter? I scanned the menu, searching for recognisable dishes, which happened to be 'Potage de Jour' and 'Befsteak.' When he had completed his next lap around the room, I ordered those. He gabbled something in French, to which I nodded, having no idea of his meaning. When the main dish arrived I realised he had asked if I wanted my steak rare, for that is how it arrived. I prefer it well done, but as it was my own stupid fault I decided not to initiate another dash to the kitchen for the poor man.

After chewing on the steak for some time I consulted the menu once more. 'Salad de Fruites' attracted my attention. I could hardly go wrong with that, I thought. Expecting a juicy bowl of mixed fruits topped with cream, I was disappointed to receive a tiny dish of fruit without cream. I must learn more about French cuisine, I told myself and give the poor fellow an easier time at breakfast.

This proved unnecessary, for the next morning's meal was self-service and even hot drinks were obtained from a complicated-looking machine. A fellow diner took pity on me and dispensed coffee from this infernal beast.

CHAPTER THREE

PRADELLES TO LA BASTIDE

A testing day's march of approximately twenty-seven kilometres (seventeen miles) was in prospect as I left Pradelles in bright sunshine. I had purchased the usual bottle of water and only fruit to eat, for I find that hot weather reduces the appetite, particularly when walking and fruit refreshes you.

I turned for a final view of the chapel and its attendant house of retreat (retirement home), formerly a hospice dating back to the Middle Ages. The hills had receded and before me lay an extensive patchwork of cultivated fields and rich meadows. The amenable track I was following was bordered by a colourful array of wild flowers, the most striking being bright red poppies, nodding their heads in the breeze. Life seemed good on that perfect morning.

The first stage of my day's walk was an easy descent to Langogne and in the distant haze I could discern the hills of Gévaudan that lay in wait for me.

I soon reached the busy main road in the valley bottom at the point where it enters the town. Beside the road stands a small information centre with another signboard relating to Le Chemin de Stevenson. Beneath it, a body lay curled up in a sleeping bag, dead to the world. Is this the fate of walkers on the GR 70, I wondered!

Crossing the Allier by the sturdy stone bridge I was conscious of reaching another landmark on my walk. Stevenson remarked that this was the point at which he walked out of the Vélay and into the region of Gévaudan. What he would not have seen as he did so are the industrial suburbs of the town that detract somewhat from the lovely setting of the sparkling Allier.

Langogne did not have the same time-honoured feel as Pradelles when I progressed along its lengthy main street, lined with modern shops and premises. This major thoroughfare is much broader than the latter's charming, narrow alleys. However, an older and more attractive street runs parallel to it. Busy market stalls lined the main square, which houses the historic Hall aux Grains, erected in 1743. This edifice would probably have been the site for selling grain. It adds character to the square and is fronted by a statue depicting a man being attacked by the fearful 'Beast of Gévaudan.' You will recall that Stevenson gave a lengthy description of the animal that ate women and children. The effigy ensures that its memory is perpetuated here, perhaps as a warning to naughty children!

Another feature in Langogne's favour is the small, but splendid ornamental fountain I discovered near the square. I also found a rather amusing display of car exhausts that completely filled a shop window, smiling at the thought of being suitably exhausted myself on reaching La Bastide!

After a brief stop for refreshment I left the town along the Avenue Joffre, which heralded two kilometres of road-walking up a demanding gradient. I observed several flocks of animals grazing in the nearby fields as I toiled, several of whom eyed me with great interest, or was it pity!

At Le Grand Champ I left the road and followed a series of paths and narrow roads through the Forest of Mercoire to the hamlet of St. Flour de Mercoire. I was still climbing and took a much-needed rest, to cool down. As I neared St. Flour I felt refreshed and eager to see if the village contained anything of note. It has several items of interest, some historical, like the menhir, a prehistoric standing stone and the ancient weather-beaten gravestones bearing family crests. An unusual monument to the fallen in the First World War displays photographs of the men who lost their lives in the conflict. The inscription reads that they were all heroes, who died for France.

The shapely and many-buttressed church has a slender bell-tower and an ancient cross close by. A more modern and surprising building is the theatre, L'Arentelle, not something you would expect to find in such a rather isolated village. It is surprising in the respect that the village lacks virtually any other amenity, such as shops, post office or café. The theatre also has two strange objects on display on its exterior. Mounted above the entrance is a vintage motor cycle, and, issuing from its exhaust, is the exclamation 'la Vie!'(Life!) Also on its wall is an inscription by the

Market and Hall Aux Grains, Langogne

celebrated writer Jean Vilar, proclaiming that theatre should be for the benefit of all, not just the elite and it performs a public service in the same way as a gas and electricity supply! I could not help feeling that food for the soul was a lot easier to obtain in St. Flour de Mercoire than food to eat!

There was no easing of the gradient as I continued through the pine forests making for the tiny settlement of Sagne-Rousse. Stevenson was relieved to reach this hamlet as it provided a landmark for him whilst searching for Cheylard L'Evêque. He had become disorientated by the maze of forest tracks and his problems were far from over at this point. He lost his way again and endured much tribulation in nearby Fouzilhic and Fouzilhac.

I found these two tiny elevated outposts virtually as he describes them. Fouzilhic, which he blundered into initially, now consists of a mere two dwellings instead of three! Fouzilhac still has the greater number.

I smiled at the thought of his dealings with their inhabitants. He had been shown kindness at Fouzilhic,

Ancient Lintel, Langogne

where the old man who had given him directions that evening was amazed to see him reappear the following morning. In contrast, the people of Fouzilhac, showed him nothing but animosity, particularly the unruly children he hoped would be eaten by the 'Beast of Gévaudan.' Thankfully, my journey through these secluded settlements was far more peaceful, but I did have the advantage of a detailed map! However, it would have been cooler whilst Stevenson was suffering his tribulations in the evening and early morning. Without the shelter of pines in that locality, I was really feeling the heat, still having covered less than half of the day's journey and with the afternoon already upon me.

Beyond Fouzilhic my route swung to the east. (I had been heading south-west since I left the road at Le Grand Champ) Following an extremely steep descent I entered Cheylard L'Evêque buried deep in a constricting hollow. It is a massive place compared to the previous three hamlets that I encountered, having all of twenty-five houses that coat the valley bottom, plus a welcome café that gave me temporary refuge and refreshment.

Stevenson was not impressed by the village, declaring that it was hardly worth searching for. Today the place is much improved, as typified by an attractive corner that contains a decorative wrought-iron cross mounted on a time-worn stone plinth. It is surrounded by tasteful mature dwellings, the finest of these being a row of neat cottages sporting brightly-painted shutters at their windows, flowers in hanging baskets and colourful parasols on their tiny patios.

The small ancient chapel stands alone amongst rock and heather, overlooked by a range of well-established firs. A figure of Our Lady stands atop its ornamental façade, as though keeping watch on the surroundings

I took the narrow road from Cheylard L'Evêque and, having dropped down into the deep valley on entering the place, I was now obliged to climb out of it, which took its toll on lungs and legs. Thankfully, after one kilometre the gradient eased and I enjoyed temporary relief until another tortuous climb faced me at Les Chabasses. Sweating brow and aching limbs were now the order of the day as I ascended the vertiginous hillside. I was beginning to wonder why I had decided to attempt such a punishing day's journey, but when I reached relatively level ground my mood improved, as did my progress.

The next stage took me through the forest of Dom de la Gardille and eventually to the village of Luc, lying in the valley of the River Allier. Stevenson was not in the best of spirits either during this section of his walk. He was still unhappy with Modestine, considering her pretty enough, but stupid and feeling that he would have to eventually carry her! The keen wind that battered them necessitated his holding onto the pack that Modestine carried with one hand all the way from Cheylard L'Evêque to Luc. He likened the area to the worst of the Scottish Highlands; cold, bare and devoid of any redeeming features. The landscape has changed in the interim years, for I was tramping through thick forest during much of this part of my journey.

Another steep descent, cutting out several bends in the

twisting road that I had recently joined, brought me in sight of the partially ruined, but impressive chateau on the outskirts of Luc. Its remains stand on a rough hillock above the village, amid a pleasing landscape of gorse, fir and ash. Today this former medieval fortress consists mainly of the restored keep and a tower that appears to be undergoing renovation. The keep has a shapely-angled roof topped by a large statue of Our Lady, who was now becoming a common sight. Thankfully, the on-going restoration ensures that an important part of the heritage of Gévaudan is being preserved.

The chateau was once of great importance in the region and suffered during the Wars of Religion and the Revolution, during which, Cardinal Richelieu ordered its demolition.

A fertile plane appeared as I left the chateau, the area being agricultural, with many people earning their living from the land. The village of Luc is reasonably large, with a population of roughly 300 and I was soon overlooking the cluster of delicate-red roofs that surround its church tower. Beyond the village, meadow and field soon gave way to the familiar rolling hills, many coated with chestnut and birch.

I found the village quite attractive, particularly its old church. Stevenson did not think much of Luc, except its chateau. He must have been having an off day, for nothing seemed to please him. Of course he had much to endure, through Modestine's antics and his difficulty in route-finding. He has my sympathy, especially regarding the seemingly endless tracks on the day's march. Forest tracks can be most confusing, especially when, at times, I arrived at a junction and had to search for the red and white waymarks. During my journey I had to backtrack several times along such tracks when waymarks seemed non-existent.

Despite Stevenson's lack of enthusiasm for the village he found the inn welcoming and decided to spend the night there. Unfortunately, this compounded the troubles of his day. Lying on straw in a box-bed and covered with merely a pair of table-napkins he shivered for most of the night and his teeth chattered. He sorely missed his sheepskin

L'Arentelle Theatre, St. Flour-de-Mercoire

sleeping sack and the lee of a great wood.

I took the C2 road from the village that soon joins the D 906, the main road running through the valley of the Allier. It was approaching evening by this time and I was still several miles from my destination, La Bastide. From the map it was apparent that most of this would be by road, which is good for route-finding, but hard on the feet.

I turned off the main road into the hamlet of Pranlac and crossed a bridge over the Allier. At this point the river marks the boundary between the departments of Lozère, to the west and Ardèche, to the east.

It was pleasant walking by the energetic infant river that rises in the nearby hills below the summit of Le Moure de la Gardille. I felt buoyed by the pleasant sun-soaked surroundings and the cool of early evening as I entered Laveyrune. In this village, which is almost an extension of Pranlac, I met several cyclists coming in the opposite direction and I came upon a checkpoint where others were taking refreshment. Colourful Lycra outfits were on display,

Chapel, Cheylard L'Evêque

in addition to fevered brows, as the cyclists snatched a brief respite.

Flags were strung across the road, bearing the names 'L'Ardechoise' and 'Rhone Alps.' This was obviously a fairly major cycle race; not on the scale of the Tour de France, but pretty gruelling. The Rhone Alps is an extensive region of south-east France, which includes the Ardèche and is based on the upper Rhone valley. Its main centres are Grenoble and Lyon, where the Rhone meets its tributary, the Saone.

I watched the cyclists, chattering excitedly, for a few minutes, before hitting the road once more towards Roglerton that lies roughly two kilometres farther along the valley. Here I met the main road once again, leading to La Bastide. I had a decision to make at this point and I made the wrong one. There was an opportunity to leave the road, which was the most direct route, and the traffic and take the GR 70 across country through the hamlet of Le Fraisse. What I didn't know at the time was that the GR 70 had been re-routed.

I should have known better than to take this longer route at the end of a gruelling day, but I blithely followed a quiet road to Le Fraisse where the red and white waymarks were conspicuous by their absence. I ground to a halt in the village, not knowing which direction to take. There was no sign of life until I met two men who lived in the locality. 'The path has been diverted,' one informed me, 'but I'll tell you how to get back on your route.' After listening to his complicated directions I joined a narrow overgrown path that descended into the valley beneath the village. Chest-high in weeds, I began to doubt the man's instructions. The path led to grassy meadows in the valley bottom where all signs of further paths disappeared. I blundered through them to find my way barred by a barbed-wire fence. Cursing my luck I retraced my steps, ready to give my so-called benefactor a piece of my mind. Unfortunately, when I returned to the village there was no sign of the two men.

There was nothing for it but to retreat to Roglerton and take the road to La Bastide. My mood was turning very sour as I retraced my steps. It was already 6-30pm and I had added an extra two kilometres to my day's journey. Fatigue began to take hold and my pace slowed as I rejoined the main road. In desperation I even thought of hitching a lift, but put the wicked thought out of my head.

Thankfully, the traffic was not heavy as I completed the last lap to La Bastide, hungry and weary. As I approached the town I saw something that raised a smile. A woolly-haired llama was grazing in a field by the roadside. When the animal noticed me it rushed to the boundary fence and began to follow me. It seemed quite aggressive and I was glad that the fence was separating us. When it reached the end of the field it tried to get over the fence and watched me intently as I left it behind.

Following this episode, signs appeared heralding the imminent arrival of La Bastide and offering accommodation. They gave the town its full title of La Bastide Puylaurent, that resides in the Lozère Department of the Languedoc-Roussillon Region.

I gave these signs scant attention as I entered the town just prior to 7-30 pm and began a search for my night's accommodation. I found it in the centre of the small town, an old-established inn overlooking the main street. Its only door opened straight into the street and it had a sparse interior with a small bar and a dining room that resembled a transport café.

A woman, who turned out to be the 'patron,' was serving behind the bar when I entered. A cigarette was dangling from her mouth, which reduced my enthusiasm for the place even more. Several locals were seated at the bar and all eyes turned pityingly in my direction. I realised that I must resemble not only an exhausted wretch, but a foreign one. Smiling apologetically, I gave the woman my name. 'Chambre douze!' (Room twelve), she said curtly, pointing to a keyboard, hanging on the wall near the entrance. 'Diner, huit heurs!' (Dinner, eight o'clock). This was evidently a woman of few words. At least I was not late for the meal, which would probably be a hanging offence!

As I removed my room key from the board I asked directions to my room. 'Premier etage!'(Second floor) she announced, 'La porte est ici!' She pointed to a nearby door. If I had not felt so weary, I would have bid her goodbye and found other accommodation, but I opened the door meekly and climbed the stairs in order to find my room that was at the end of a dark passage. Unable to find the light switch I groped my way along peering at room numbers on the doors. When I entered my room I found that although it contained a miniscule shower, there was no toilet. By this time I could not have cared if it did not have a ceiling. It had a bed, a wardrobe and washbasin and I was ready to sleep anywhere. When I eventually found the toilet, it was at the end of another dark corridor, with barely enough room to sit down! At last I mastered the light switches, which, I discovered were controlled by a timer, so one had to move quickly if you did not wish to be plunged into darkness.

I just had time for a quick shower before dinner loomed. What if it was served by 'Sybil Faulty,' as I had dubbed the patron? I did not wish to be ejected from Faulty Towers for failure to learn her language! Sadly, there was no time for swatting up on French cuisine.

A shock awaited me as I arrived in the dining room. It was full of cyclists, taking part in a rally through the region, but they were no relation to the racing cyclists I had encountered in Laveyrune. The dreaded patron was busy serving plates heaped with salad, liberally laced with olive oil and mayonnaise and covered with diced vegetables. She pointed to a small table in the corner and I sat down, wondering what fate had in store. A plate of salad was soon thrust under my nose, indicating that there was no choice of menu. By that time I was ready to eat anything and relieved that I need not worry about ordering any dishes.

The substantial helping of salad on my plate was filling enough, but when the main course arrived I gulped. It was a large braised leg of lamb accompanied by vegetables and a great heap of what resembled small pieces of macaroni. The cyclists were attacking their portions with gusto so I waded in, just managing to finish mine as 'Sybil Faulty' arrived with the cheese board. Should I decline? Memories of walking in Scotland with my companion, Maurice, re-surfaced. At a bed and breakfast establishment one evening he had the temerity to refuse a huge slice of gateau after consuming a plate of salmon, potatoes and vegetables that would have floored a navvy. Our hostess was horrified and asked indignantly if he did not care for her cooking. To keep the peace with 'Sybil,' I had two small portions of cheese.

The dessert that followed was mercifully not substantial. It suited my sweet tooth, for it consisted of jam, covered with thin custard and topped with cream; sickly, but pleasant.

Having survived the meal I crawled back to my room and went straight to bed.

CHAPTER FOUR

LA BASTIDE TO NOTRE DAME DES NEIGES

Next day was a rest day, so to speak. I planned to walk a mere four kilometres to the monastery where Stevenson had spent several days during his journey and return to La Bastide for a second night.

After my energetic days of walking, I slept soundly until 6am when I was awakened by the cyclists running water taps and flushing the toilet. At 8am I went down for breakfast, as instructed, to find that the cyclists had departed and I was left on my own. Food was arranged on the bar, behind which was the patron and a man I assumed was either her husband, or the cook. The fellow had wandered from table to table the previous evening inquiring if the meal was satisfactory. He was a man of few words, in contrast to his wife, as I discovered later that he was, in fact, her husband. Poor chap, he probably could not get a word in when his wife was around.

I began to help myself to crockery and the food arranged on the bar, which, fortunately, included a supply of 'Kelloggs.' However, when I began to pour the only milk in view onto my cornflakes, 'Sybil' cried, 'C'est pour le café!' (That is for the coffee!) Abashed, I nearly dropped the jug, I watched compliantly as she opened a carton of milk, which she handed to me with a scowl.

After breakfast I informed 'Sybil' that I was visiting the monastery of Notre Dame des Neiges (Our Lady of the Snows). 'Laisse votre clef!' (Leave your key!) I was commanded as she pointed to the keyboard.

I left around 9am, not wishing to spend more time in my room than was necessary. The route by road is shorter than the meandering alternative and I chose that as the traffic was very light. I walked slowly not wishing to arrive before 10am, the time that I assumed the monastery would be opened to the public.

I was eager to see the place where Stevenson had spent several days taking in its routines and conversing with other boarders. As I walked through an avenue of trees towards

Notre Dame des Neiges - Monks at Worship

the entrance it appeared very different to what I had imagined. I had expected an old and rambling establishment, but it proved to be a complex of modern-looking buildings scattered amongst extensive and impressive tree-studded grounds. I discovered that the monastery that Stevenson had known was destroyed by fire in 1912. It was rebuilt in two years, thanks to the sterling efforts of the abbot and his community. Further renewal and transformation was carried out during the abbacy of Dom Claudius Valour (1952-1982), who oversaw the construction of the guesthouse and the renovation of the monastery, in addition to the premises used to receive the numerous guests and those on retreat at the abbey.

A map situated at the entrance identifies the various buildings within the complex. In addition to the abbey there is a visitor section, church, small chapel, hotel and even an up to date video theatre.

There was no sign of other visitors when I arrived and I began to examine the buildings situated by the entrance, as

The Library

the reception appeared to be unmanned. As I walked I came across a nearby garden, in which one of the monks was working. He saw me and gave a friendly wave, but did not speak. He was dressed in a plain grey habit, which, I assumed was his working attire, for many others wore the traditional black and white garments.

A sign denoting the video display centre caught my eye and I entered the building. An elderly monk appeared from an office by the door. He spoke no English, but appeared friendly and helpful. I asked if I could view the video and he nodded, returning to the office for a key. He led me to the door of the theatre, which he unlocked and ushered me inside. The place was well-designed and modern with amply raked seating. I had the pick of the seats, being the only occupant, the monk having disappeared into the projector room to start the video.

The performance lasted for half an hour and illustrates life at the abbey. I was very impressed with its quality and hoped that many visitors took advantage of it. No one else entered during the performance and when I left I called at the office to thank the kindly monk, who smiled and shook my hand.

According to the video, life has changed little at the monastery since Stevenson's visit. The daily routine is the same as that led by all monks and nuns of the Cistercian order. The first bell sounds at 4am (Stevenson mentions it sounding at 2 am) signifying time for the first Office, that of the Vigils. This is the first of seven communal gatherings for prayer, to sing the Eucharist or to sing the praise of God, throughout the day and evening. The mass is the centre and heart of the monastic day. Meetings for communal worship are interspersed with private prayer and daily tasks. The latter extend from the kitchen and the garden to the infirmary and the reception, whilst also encompassing other services required by a variety of needs.

Tasks can also include the work through which the community makes its living. According to his aptitudes each monk can play a part in this, be it working in the wine cellar, the farm or the workshops. This is just as in Stevenson's time when he refers to each brother being able to choose his occupation, in addition to his religious duties and general labours.

Throughout the years the brotherhood has been self-sufficient and today, more than ever, this is aided by facilities for visitors. The video display is one such, and although no charge is made any gifts of money are gratefully accepted. There is a small café and a shop selling souvenirs, assorted gifts and books. Also, a small museum, to which entry is free, but all donations are welcome. The hotel caters for visitors, who should apply to the 'Frère Hôtelier' for meals and accommodation.

A large source of income is derived from the sale of wine that is left to mature in large vats in the winery. It is distributed to local towns and villages and is also sold in the abbey shop.

You will recall that Stevenson incurred the wrath of a priest and a former soldier, who were fellow boarders at the monastery. During their discussions they were alarmed by Stevenson's heretical views, as they perceived them to be. I had no such problems and was able to wander around the grounds at will and visit parts of the complex.

This I began following the appearance of several visitors, who seemed intent on doing the same. The small, but delightful chapel with its tiny bell tower was my first port of call. Standing in the shadow of the abbey, this small stone-built place of worship is ultra modern. It possesses but a few small windows and its interior was in darkness as I entered. Gradually, my eyes became accustomed to the conditions and I was able to switch on several spotlights to reveal its plain rendered walls and wooden roof trusses. The furnishing is sparse with bare wooden benches lining each side-wall and several small stools are scattered around. A basic stone altar stands, in the shadow of a simple wooden cross, on a shallow platform at one end of the building. A little light filtered through the windows that are decorated with abstract, but tasteful patterns. These unadorned surroundings demonstrate the simple life that a monk leads, dedicated to prayer and the casting aside of worldly possessions.

The abbey itself is the highest in France at approximately 1,128 metres (3,700 feet). It is a majestic building with a prominent clock tower that can be seen from a considerable distance. Its stonework, like that of the abbey church, is in pristine condition. A small ornamental garden provides an attractive frontage to the building and emerald lawns surround it and the adjacent white-walled hotel.

After my tour of the grounds I returned to entrance and noticed that the attractive courtyard that gives access to the museum, cafe and boutique (shop) had been opened to visitors. I entered to find that, like many of the other buildings, its surrounding walls are pleasing white stucco and contain numerous shapely arches. The centre-piece of the courtyard is a neatly manicured lawn edged with a scattering of olive and chestnut trees. A darker green ring of fir and pine protrudes above the red roof, a reminder that the monastery is set in a clearing amidst an extensive forest.

I called in the café for some refreshment, but found that it provided drinks only. I ordered coffee, which is served black, the alternatives being wine or fruit juice.

The Wine Cellar

A little later I looked around the museum that contained a display dedicated to the memory of Charles de Foucauld, who was accepted as a novice in 1890. He had been a cavalry officer and was converted to the faith in 1886. His first stay at Notre Dame des Neiges lasted only several months as he soon left for Akbès, a priory in Syria, founded in 1881 by Abbot Polycarp. The abbot and his flock, persecuted by the Republican government at that time, took refuge there having vacated Notre Dame des Neiges. Charles spent seven years in either the monastery or the priory. In 1900, after living alone in Palestine, he returned to the monastery to study in preparation for his priestly ordination, which took place in 1901. A year later he left for the Sahara, where a tragic death awaited him in 1916. Although much travelled, Charles always retained a great affection for Notre Dame des Neiges, which inspired him to perform many good works.

Before leaving the monastery I visited the shop and purchased several items. The brother who served me spoke

The Printing Room

a little and told me that brethren who have regular contact with visitors are permitted to break their silence. Other monks I encountered during my visit did not speak at all, thus observing their order's vow of silence.

I had expected more visitors to the monastery, but there were few in evidence before 1pm, when I left. Returning to La Bastide by the same route, I found all the shops and restaurants closed. Searching for somewhere to eat, I eventually found a small café on the outskirts that was open. There was not a soul around when I entered and I wondered if this establishment was also closed. I was on the point of leaving when, to my relief, a man appeared from the kitchen. It took all my linguistic skill to inquire if the place was open and if so could I have a light meal? The man merely smiled. I repeated my request, believing that he had not understood my meaning. Silence once more. As we stood looking at each other, a woman, who I took to be his wife, entered. I found that she spoke a little English.

'Pardon my husband, he cannot speak,' she said apologetically. It took all my willpower to keep a straight face, for I realised that I, with my pigeon French, had been trying to converse with a Frenchman who was dumb!

The woman indicated a table and I sat down. As I did so she hurriedly retired to the kitchen before returning and kneeling beside the table. What kind of place is this, I wondered? Then I grasped what she was doing. She was folding a piece of paper, which she was about to slide under a leg of the table. I rocked the table and found that she was placing it under the wrong leg! I pointed to another leg and she placed it under, saying 'Merci' (Thank you). I gave her the 'thumbs up' sign and she smiled.

I indicated that I only required a snack - I had still to face another of 'Sybil's' gigantic meals that evening - and could she suggest anything? She offered crêpes (pancakes), with strawberry preserve, which seemed to fit the bill and I nodded.

Whilst she was preparing them in the kitchen I smiled at the thought of the little cameo that had been played out in that deserted café.

The pancakes were very tasty and when I came to pay the bill the woman inquired if I was just passing through the town. I mentioned 'Le Chemin de Stevenson' that most French people with which I came into contact recognised immediately. She seemed impressed and wished me well.

What to do for the rest of the afternoon, I wondered? I was eager to be on my way once more, but all my accommodation was pre-booked, which included the two night's stay in La Bastide. I wandered around the centre of town, gazing in shop windows, which I eventually tired of and strolled into a local park to sit on a bench. The weather was maintaining its high standard and it was pleasant relaxing in the sun, the only disturbance coming from some youths playing football.

Eventually, a local man approached and asked if he could join me. He spoke English and after the usual question regarding my travels the conversation turned to his hometown. La Bastide, he explained, had virtually faded back into the surrounding forests after World War Two. It subsisted temporarily on the custom from rail workers and a local dam-building project. This, however, could not stem its decline and the winter population dropped to a mere 183. In the summer it swelled to 2000 with extra rail staff and villa owners from the surrounding centres of Marseilles, Alais, Nimes and Montpelier. Each year fewer residents stayed during the winter and the railway branch line to Mende began to lose money. This posed a serious threat, for if it closed, La Bastide might have disappeared from the map. Mercifully, the GR 70 was established and numerous walkers like myself began to arrive along the Allier in Stevenson's footsteps. The situation is now much improved and the local economy has been swelled by the influx of tourists and walkers.

We enjoyed a very interesting conversation until the man informed me that the shops would be opening and he needed some supplies. I thanked him for his company and strolled around the park, eventually crossing a footbridge over the sun-dappled Allier, its waters tinkling over a stony bed. I then joined an inviting looking field path. Things went well until the path became overgrown and I found my way barred by a barbed-wire fence. Not wishing to backtrack, I foolishly climbed over the fence, fell over and grazed my shin quite badly. I cursed my ill fortune, hoping that my injury would not impede my progress on the following day. I had some dressings amongst my first aid supplies that I carried with me and when I eventually returned to the inn, I dressed the angry-looking wound.

CHAPTER FIVE

LA BASTIDE TO LE BLEYMARD

The following morning the weather remained fine and a good day seemed in prospect. My route directions indicated that the day's walk would be twenty-four kilometres (fifteen miles), but it turned out to be far more rigorous than I anticipated. I left the town at 9am. It was Sunday and surprisingly, all the shops were open. Instead of purchasing my day's supplies I decided to wait until I reached Chasseradès, which proved a bad move.

The initial part of my route followed the D906 road once more as it threads through the extensive forests that form part of the Ardèche Mountains Nature Park. It was a gradual climb to the hamlet of Le Thort and as I approached the village I entered open countryside. I was treated to some fine long-distance views over rolling hills, some of their gentle slopes carpeted with conifers.

I followed a minor road through Le Thort and on its outskirts I passed a 'dolmen,' known as 'The Giant's Palette.' This is a massive round stone, reputedly 5,000 years old that would have formed the roof of a Megalithic tomb. These flat stones were laid on top of substantial upright ones, to form a prodigious burial chamber.

A little farther along the road I made a miscalculation. A track forked to the left and I noticed the familiar red and white waymark. Thinking this would be a chance to get off the road I started along it. All went well initially as I followed it downhill, watching my step on its rough ribbed schist-like surface. I was to encounter much more of the glinting silvery rock during the next few days. Hemmed in by trees and bushes, I continued to watch where I was placing my feet until I came to a clearing, where I was treated to an inspiring spectacle. A magnificent landscape unfolded before me revealing what I would encounter over the next two days. In the distance lay the forest of La Goulet that coats a formidable mountain barrier and beyond, the dark brooding mass that is the Mont Lozère range dominated the skyline. The summit of Mont Lozère forms the highest point of Stevenson's journey, at 1,699 metres (5,572 feet).

After elation came disappointment. Occasionally glancing at the stimulating view, I continued my descent until doubt entered my mind. It appeared that I was walking into the wrong valley and had veered off course. I checked my map and, to my dismay, I found that this was the case. I was walking part of the GR 72 instead of the GR 70. I should have kept to the road!

There was nothing for it but to backtrack, which cost a valuable three-quarters of an hour. So much for my short day!

At Le Croix de Peyre, one of several ancient crosses in the area, another waymarked path left the road, but after my experience with the previous one I was determined to keep to tarmac all the way to Chasseradès. This I did and was compensated by a lovely panorama as I approached the tiny picture postcard outpost of Les Gouttes, set deep in a charming cleft amidst the hills.

I followed the snaking road past the hamlet of Grossefage and onwards to its junction with the D6 that led me to the ancient and picturesque village of Chasseradès. The church with its stately tower dominates the surroundings as you approach. As I passed between the time-worn stucco walls of its buildings, enlivened by colourful hanging baskets and window boxes, time appeared to have passed this little enclave by. Its streets form a veritable warren of antiquity and I imagine Stevenson would have probably seen the village in the same light. He arrived here at sundown and made for the inn, which he found full of men occupied in surveying a projected railway through the locality. Nevertheless, he enjoyed their company and spent an enlightening evening listening to their tales whilst drinking a good amount of hot wine. They retired to bed at a late hour and he found himself sharing a bedroom once again, this time with five of the railway surveyors. Generously, he was given a bed to himself and the others had to share the remaining three.

Stevenson was not so lucky the following morning when

Station, La Bastide

he was wakened at 5am by shouts to his companions that it was time to begin work for the day.

Pride of place in Chasseradès must be given to the church, which perches on a hilltop and is in pristine condition. Apart from its splendid tower, it does not have the appearance of a conventional church, as other buildings, which I imagine are dwellings, are attached to it. However, this does not detract from its appeal and I believe that Stevenson would have been inspired to make a sketch of the delightful place of worship. When I left the village it remained imprinted in my memory.

Another memorable feature of Chasseradès is the venerable pair of stone washhouses, where the women of the village came to do their washing and, presumably, enjoy a good chat with their fellow villagers. Beautifully preserved, these agreeable structures resemble gigantic dog kennels.

This was becoming a most enjoyable section of my journey, as I followed two walkers down the steep descent

Washouses - Chasseradès

to the hamlet of Mirandol. A fine vista of luxuriant meadows and the steeply inclined forest of La Goulet lay on the far side of the scenic valley.

The cottages of tiny Mirandol shelter beneath a tall railway viaduct, which equals the grandeur of that at Arquejols. It spans the yawning valley in a broad curve before passing through one of several stone-built snow sheds that resemble miniature tunnels. The line is one of the highest in France, reaching 1,219 metres (4,000 feet); hence the protection from snow.

I walked beneath the mighty arches of the viaduct and into the compact settlement, past mature stone dwellings and roadside verges adorned with wild flowers and cherry-red rose bushes. At this point I nearly caught up with the pair of walkers I had followed from Chasseradès. They seemed uncertain of their route and, as they disappeared from view around a corner, I spied a red and white GR 70 waymark. Assuming they were following the same route as me, I shouted, but received no reply. However, a few minutes later I found them behind me and realised they had taken a roundabout course.

The track I was following deteriorated into a narrow path hemmed in by vegetation. It meandered through meadows until it reached the railway line, which it ran alongside to another small village, L'Estampe.

By this time I was quite hungry, having found no shops in Chasseradès or Mirandol. Why had I not purchased food and water in La Bastide? My water had run out because of the hot conditions, but I had a slab of gingerbread, muesli bars and chocolate bars in my pack in case of emergency. I sorely needed a fresh supply of water, but L'Estampe proved shopless too. This was a serious dilemma, for I faced a stiff climb over La Goulet in the afternoon heat. However, salvation was at hand, for I passed a couple sitting in the garden of their cottage and asked if they knew where I could obtain water. The woman led me to a nearby tap with a notice above it declaring 'L'eau potable' (Water drinkable). Very relieved, I thanked the woman and replenished my water bottle, which, it transpired, was sorely needed during the forthcoming climb.

Stevenson found the village quite a busy place. He had difficulty negotiating the narrow main street, for he found it completely blocked with sheep. From the surrounding fields he heard the strident note of a shepherd's horn and the ringing of cowbells as he left.

Today it is a quieter spot. Apart from the fore-mentioned couple, I met only one other person and noticed a few sheep in the fields as I passed through.

My tussle with La Goulet began shortly after joining the meandering road on the outskirts of the village. The gradient began to stiffen and I soon left the road to join a track that ascended through birch woods.

I laboured up the steep and winding thoroughfare into the depths of the forest. Thankfully, it was waymarked in the red and white of the GR 70 and also the GR 7A. How glad I was of the water, for sweat was pouring from me.

After a while two cyclists passed me as they strained up the punishing slope. I admired their tenacity, for they had

Cairns on La Goulet

the stony surface of the track to contend with in addition to
the climb. The stronger of the two was in the lead and he was
obliged to keep stopping to wait for his companion.
Consequently, I passed them several times, which gave my
flagging spirits a lift.

After a long struggle I approached a col on the main ridge
and had just rejoined the road when thunderclaps began and
gradually increased in volume, signifying that I was in for a
soaking. When they rumbled overhead the heavens opened
and I sheltered under the welcome foliage of fir by the
roadside. The storm lasted for fifteen minutes and when it
had abated I was able to push on towards the summit. When
I finally reached my goal, at 1,413 metres (4,635 feet), I sank
to the ground, ignoring the damp conditions. In celebration
I ate some more of the tasty gingerbread washed down with
plenty of water.

After this respite I felt a little more human and checked
my watch. It was late afternoon, which persuaded me to
pick the more direct of the two possible routes that lead

down the other side of the mountain to the village of Les Alpiers. Both routes thread through the forest along contorted tracks, the road having departed at the summit. Thus began a protracted descent with all views blotted out, which was not a great misfortune, for angry black clouds hovered overhead. They were a portent of what transpired some minutes later. Hailstones, the size of five pence coins rained down on me like bullets. I dived for cover under the trees whilst the track I was following began to resemble a ski slope

Eventually, I was able to emerge from my hiding place and resume my descent. Stevenson met a solitary traveller with a bullock cart during his downward climb, but I met no one. The cyclists had disappeared, along the road I presumed.

The wind was quite strong and it began to dry my sodden walking jacket and trousers. It had been effective by the time I emerged from the forest, for they were nearly dry. I could see Les Alpiers beneath me, sheltering on the edge of the clearing. Stevenson had taken in the view from here of the Lozère range across the valley, which he described as, 'well enough modelled on the flanks, but straight and dull in outline.'

The clouds were very low as I surveyed the scene and they blotted out much of my surroundings. Ignoring the deterioration in the weather, I had other things on my mind. My first priority was to gather strength for the final stretch of the day's journey. I should have taken more notice of Les Alpiers as I passed through, but my thoughts were on a search for a suitable place to take a brief rest and the remaining two kilometres I still had to walk.

Eventually, I found a convenient wall to sit on, where I demolished the remaining gingerbread and ate a muesli bar as I thought about Stevenson's tribulations during his ascent of the Goulet. Tired of traversing the severely winding road as it climbed from L'Estampe, he decided to cut out the loops and take a short cut up the steep hillside. I smiled at the thought of his tussle with Modestine, who would have none of it, resisting his goad, and braying loudly in protest. Once again, it made me appreciate that I was walking alone, unencumbered by a belligerent donkey. On second thoughts, the fatigue I was feeling would probably have led me to ride the animal!

Hitching on my pack I left gloomy Les Alpiers and began a gradual descent, which deteriorated into an abrupt rocky decline as I neared Le Bleymard. I clambered carefully down the extremely rough track towards the village nestling deep in the seemingly remote valley. Obeying Wainwright's instructions to always look where you are putting your feet I resisted the temptation to gaze into the green amphitheatre that lay beneath me whilst on the move. I did, however, stop occasionally to admire the vibrant green of the meadows surrounding the tree-encircled village.

In the valley bottom, with my bones thankfully intact, I joined the D901 road, which Stevenson mentions as the 'high road.' that links Villefort with Mende. It was a short distance from there to the Hotel La Remise, conveniently situated by the roadside. Like my accommodation in La Bastide, it had the appearance of an old inn and an array of inviting tables lined the pavement outside. I was later to discover that it was, in fact, an ancient coaching inn, located at the meeting of two old 'chemin de muletiers' (packhorse routes).

As soon as I entered I had a good feeling about the place. Its interior had been modernised, but with good taste and without the destruction of many of its original features. It was an inn that retained its character. I peeped into the dining room to find it far more impressive than 'Sybil's.' My room was comfortable, with en suite facilities. No creeping along corridors to the toilet required here!

Before taking a shower I examined the wound on my leg that had not troubled me, thankfully, during the day's walk. When I removed the dressing I found it had wept slightly, but otherwise looked satisfactory.

The meal that evening was splendid and I was fortunate to meet a fellow Englishman who was touring the area by car. When I explained that I was attempting the GR 70 he declared that walking to the end of the road from his house was enough exercise for him!

CHAPTER SIX

LE BLEYMARD TO LE PONT DE MONTVERT

Mont Lozère day! According to Stevenson I was to face the sternest test of all, the ascent of the challenging mountain. He had two bites of the cherry, as it were, for he scaled the foothills of the Lozère before camping overnight and heading for the summit the following morning. Before leaving Le Bleymard that evening he had dined at an inn. Could it be the one at which I stayed, I wondered?

The storms of the previous day appeared to have unsettled the weather, for that morning I set out beneath a grey sky. Every cloud has a silvery lining, I reckoned, for it would most likely be cool during my ascent of the mountain.

I crossed the bridge over the River Lot, one of France's most celebrated rivers and reached the memorial to Henri Rouviere. It is in the form of an impressive stone obelisk with a representation of Henri's head carved on it. The obelisk stands in miniature garden ringed by colorful blooms and shrubbery. From there I followed the red and white waymarks into the town-centre and through its maze of narrow streets, where the route became hard to follow. It is often the case that the most difficult part of navigation is finding your way from a town or village. The waymarks had disappeared and I spent thirty minutes wandering the outskirts trying to discover the correct path. At one stage I mistakenly took a dead-end road that ended at the cemetery and had to backtrack.

Eventually, I found the desired path and climbed the steep hillside, which afforded good views over the verdant valley of the Lot. I joined a wide track, which I assumed is the ancient drove road that Stevenson took. My surroundings were free of the ubiquitous trees as I ascended to Col Santel and the gradient was not severe. However, things changed at the col, for I entered the forest of Charamasse and the track became steeper. As I toiled up it the surface became stonier and my progress slowed. A young couple caught up with me. They spoke perfect

View to La Goulet and Mont Lozère Range

Chasseradès – Church

Chasseradès

Railway Viaduct – Mirandol

Le Bleymard

Chalet du Mont Lozère (Ski Station)

Finiels

Le Pont de Montvert

Le Pont de Montvert – du Chayla's House

Le Pont de Montvert – Les Cévennes Hotel

View from the ridge near Col de La Planette

Florac

Florac

St. Germain de Calberte – Cévenoles Memorial

St. Etienne Vallée Française

St. Jean du Gard

English and I discovered that their home was in Amsterdam. Like the Australians I met at Arlempdes, they had walked several long-distance paths in Britain. We kept company for a while before they forged ahead and I decided to take a rest to cool down. My expectation of cool conditions had not materialised, for it was decidedly humid.

As I was about to sit down in a clearing, a party of around thirty walkers appeared and joined me. Their leader, Jacques, told me that they all lived in Le Puy and were walking the GR 70. As we talked we noticed two donkeys grazing on the edge of the clearing and went over to them. The animals were very tame and let us stroke them. Several members of the walking party were taking photographs of the pair and Jacques suggested that he take a shot, with my camera, of me standing beside one of the animals, which I agreed to gladly. Where they had come from and who owned them? We agreed it was a mystery. How strange it was to find them in the heart of a forest. Perhaps they were following in Modestine's footsteps, we joked.

I bade the party goodbye and continued up the 'long drag' that the ascent was developing into. After what seemed an age, although I had travelled a mere nine kilometres since leaving Le Bleymard, the ground levelled and the trees receded. The welcome sight of the holiday village and ski station of Le Chalet du Mont Lozère appeared. It is a refuge of habitation and winter sport on the bare upper slopes of the mountain, lying under the shadow of the ski lift that transports skiers to the summit ridge. The complex comprises a hotel, several chalets, a shop, two restaurants and an ecumenical chapel. The latter was built in 1967 with the faith and energy of the boy-scout movement.

It seemed a convenient place for rest and refreshment before the push to the summit. To avoid the previous day's error, I had purchased food and water in Le Bleymard before setting out. During my respite I was obliged to put on my walking jacket, as it became noticeably cooler under a darkening grey sky.

I had been warned not to attempt the summit, 'Sommet de Finiels,' (which Stevenson referred to as 'Pic de Finiels') in bad weather, which seemed imminent. A decision had to

Le Bleymard

be made to take either the safer route over the Col de Finiels, or risk the summit route. I chose the latter, for Stevenson had described the remarkable views from it that stretched to the Mediterranean.

On leaving the village I walked past the chapel and began the testing climb to a col on the summit ridge. The temperature dropped further as I toiled through an ever-bleaker moorland landscape dotted with stunted trees and bushes. The well-worn track was marked with ancient upright stones that Stevenson had used as route-finders on both La Goulet and Mont Lozère. I had not encountered those of the former, but the one's I was following proved to be a godsend. As I neared the col the mist descended and reduced the visibility to twenty yards. I had to laugh. Here I was, approaching the pinnacle of my journey and the mist had arrived, exactly on cue!

To turn back would be the cowardly way out, I reckoned. I had walked in mist countless times and I had map and compass. I pushed onwards to the col and the mist

One of the Ancient Stones on Mont Lozère

thickened. When I attained the summit ridge the stones guided me to a GR 70 waymarker pointing in the direction of the summit. I left the track and joined a barely discernable path, having taken a compass bearing. This was beneficial, for there were no other navigation aids.

Just as I was beginning to think I would never reach the summit a rude shelter of loose stones appeared from the swirling mist. Inside it huddled four young French walkers studying a map and discussing the route to take off the mountain. One of them spoke English and explained that they were on a circular walk around the region. To prove that I had attained the summit of Mont Lozère I took a mist-shrouded photograph of them and the shelter. The features were barely recognisable when it was developed!

One thing puzzled me. Where was the triangulation column that normally marks a summit? I left the shelter and began a search for it. I found the column near at hand, obscured by the mist, particularly as it was a much smaller version of those in our country. Barely two feet tall, it was hardly noticeable amidst a scattering of stones.

When I returned to the shelter the Frenchmen were hoisting heavy rucksacks, with tents attached, onto their backs. They were obviously backpacking, which provides flexibility of route, but requires strength to transport the heavy load. I felt a wimp in comparison as I had the comfort of hotel accommodation.

After their departure I rested for a while in the shelter before taking another compass bearing and venturing into the mist once more. There was no sign of a path on the bare stone-riddled summit, but in a short time I found the one I was searching for. The thought crossed my mind that I was more at home in these conditions than when threading through a maze of forest paths. In fact, I had less route-finding problems crossing Mont Lozère than I had experienced whilst trying to leave Le Bleymard!

My elation soon turned to frustration when the path I was following turned into a deeply rutted and rocky obstacle course. My relief was palpable when I finally reached a forest road, still shrouded in mist. About an hour's distance from the summit I finally emerged from the murk, but all I could see was the encircling conifers.

I passed a forest shelter, handy in bad weather or if blisters became unbearable.

At last I was free of the interminable forest and I joined a dead-end road that leads to the sequestered outpost of Finiels. My spirits rose with the onset of an impressive and most welcome vista. Beneath a heavy blanket of cloud I could see the moorland flank of Mont Lozère descending into a deep fissure, the shapely valley that runs down to Le Pont de Montvert.

I had a spring in my step as I took the narrow winding road to Finiels. I had conquered Mont Lozère and was clear of the pervading forest. To add to my pleasure the sun came out as though welcoming me to this bright little settlement, bordered by oak and spruce. What a view the villagers must enjoy from their elevated perch. As I entered the neat and tidy village a sign indicating cheese for sale caught my eye. Would that be goat's cheese I wondered? The terrain was most suitable for the mountain variety. There would be, for

Le Pont de Montvert

certain, a good supply of cow's milk for cheese-making, judging by the number of cowsheds identified on the map of the area.

The buildings of Finiels cluster at the head of the valley of the Rieumalet that tumbles down to meet the Tarn at Le Pont de Montvert. I enjoyed a very pleasant interlude following its course through the hamlets of Prat Soutayran and Champlong de Lozere. The views across the attractive defile were a revelation after the mist and forests of Mont Lozère. The valley sides were strewn with large stones and sizeable rocks and tiny streams fell energetically into the infant river at frequent intervals. Stevenson found the valley so invigorating he was moved to declare, 'I have never seen a river of so changeful and delicate a hue; crystal was not more clear, the meadows not by half so green.'

As I neared Le Pont de Montvert I overlooked an even deeper gorge, where the valleys of the Ruiemalet and the Tarn meet. The valley bottoms are thickly coated with trees, which almost obscure the buildings of the town that is

121

encircled by abrupt mountainous slopes.

Le Pont de Montvert did not disappoint. It is a splendid historic town, much as Stevenson described it. The houses clinging to the hillside and the labyrinth of narrow alleyways are still to be found, the only addition being new buildings on its outskirts. The place retains a period charm, particularly the delightful bridge, after which the town is named. This curvaceous ancient structure is a focal point for the hoards of visitors. Its attractiveness is enhanced by the venerable tower that graces one end of it. The weather-beaten stone, almost the colour of straw, gives the tower a changeless appearance. Mounted on its shapely roof is a bell that has, presumably, tolled for the people of Le Pont de Montvert for centuries.

The sparkling River Tarn flows alongside the main street and under the narrow, high-arched bridge, to its meeting with the Rieumalet. As it does so, it provides a glorious opportunity for photographers.

Le Pont de Montvert lies within the Cévennes National Park that stretches from Mont Lozère to the 1,565 metres (5,133 feet) peak of Mont Aigoual in the south of the region. It is an area of extensive rich woodland, luxuriant meadows, gurgling streams, vibrant rivers and quiet roads. It also is the country of the Camisards, mainly isolated and bearing the scars of the turmoil described by Stevenson, who relates that the rebellion of the Protestant Camisards, or Cévenoles, began in Le Pont de Montvert. He appears to have been greatly moved by the tales he heard concerning the bloody and protracted conflict and the fact that it still weighed upon the minds of the people with which he came in contact.

Stevenson mentions du Chayla's house that was set alight by the avenging Camisards and I was keen to discover if it still existed. To this end I visited the National Park Centre in the main street. There I found a very helpful young lady, who spoke fluent English. She directed me to the site of his house, since rebuilt, which overlooks the junction of the Tarn and the Rieumalet. Although the house itself has changed, the terraced garden into which he leapt and was subsequently captured is still in existence. I too had been intrigued by the plight of the Camisards and, as I gazed at the house from the bridge that spans the Rieumalet I was exhilarated to see the very spot where the vile archpriest was brought to heel.

The lady also pointed out the inn, now a hotel, where Stevenson had lunch and spent an enjoyable interlude in the company of a number of local people who he found outgoing and entertaining. It is now called Les Cévennes Hotel and is a popular tourist attraction.

My accommodation was in a pleasant setting, with a balcony overlooking the Tarn. The woman at the reception desk showed me to my room and brought a smile to my face. She gave me a curtsy; a practice I thought was reserved for nobility and royalty these days!

The hotel was crowded that evening, mainly because the walking party I had met earlier in the day was staying. At dinner I listened to their loud and excited chatter that filled the dining room. The guests were served by a couple I took to be the proprietors, who were rushing between kitchen and tables like 'Nureyev' at the hotel in Pradelles. As I was on my own I was more or less ignored until the man came eventually to take my order. A short time later the woman did the same and seemed most put out when I explained that I had already ordered. She never spoke to me again. A long interval elapsed before my first course appeared and I was the last to be served the subsequent courses, having to wait whilst the walking party was given first priority.

As I was feeling tired after my strenuous day, I retired to my room after dinner, which was fairly comfortable, but not to the standard of the previous night's accommodation. I checked my leg wound before having a shower and it still looked in decent condition. On the minus side, my first blister had appeared between two toes, albeit a small one. Thankfully, it was the only one I suffered and gave me no more trouble.

I went to bed early and lay thinking of the day's happenings, particularly the mist on the upper reaches of Mont Lozère and the delightful descent through the picturesque valley of the Rieumalet. It had been a most satisfying day.

CHAPTER SEVEN

LE PONT DE MONTVERT TO FLORAC

Stevenson had followed the beautiful Tarn Gorge to Florac, my next destination, but I was to suffer disappointment in this respect. I had been informed by the young lady in the National Park Centre that it was now out of the question. Sadly, the footbridges have gone and the route is impassable for walkers. Instead of the direct route westwards through the valley, the GR 70 heads south, climbing to Col de la Planette, where it turns to the west along an extensive ridge before descending to Florac. This detour adds nine kilometres to the day's journey.

Whilst purchasing food at the boulangerie that morning I met two elderly Frenchmen, who were also walking the GR 70. One of them broke a large French stick in half, declaring it was too much for his stomach. He offered one half to me and I accepted it with thanks. I wished them bon voyage as they departed and hoped that we would meet again.

The weather was dull as I began an extremely laborious climb from Le Pont de Montvert along a winding track that took me high on the valley side before levelling out and contouring the precipitous slope. What I assumed would be impressive views were blotted out unfortunately by the leaden sky, but I pushed onwards until the track descended to a narrow dead-end road at the point where it enters the expansive Forest of Domaniale. I followed this road to its end, where I encountered Chamlong de Bougès, an ancient and former forest house set in a clearing. This seemed a good place to take a short rest.

Another steep and sweat inducing climb took me to the crest of the ridge at Col de la Planette. In a stony clearing stand several tall cairns, constructed with flat jagged stones. These are quite common in the locality and there is a tradition that you add small stones to them to signify your passage. We have a similar practice in this country of adding stones to cairns on fell and mountain summits.

The route now turns west, but the climb continued to the Signal (Beacon) de Bougès, the highest point of the Bougès

Signal de Bougès

Massif, at 1,421 metres (4,660 feet.) A large mass of ancient ragged rock beside the track I was following provided an excellent vantage-point The grey blanket of mist was beginning to thin as I scanned an unfolding panorama of mountain ridges, stretching into the far distance. It was akin to gazing over an ocean, for the dark-green tree-covered slope immediately beneath me heralded rows of blue wave crests receding into the distant haze. I was reminded of Stevenson's description of the view from the summit of Mont Lozère that I was unfortunately denied. He describes it as 'a view into the hazy air of heaven and a land of intricate blue hills below my feet.'

This spot would probably have been ideal as a lookout station and encampment for the Camisards. Stevenson mentions that they had one such on the summit of Mont Lozère. At that time the bands of Protestant outlaws had many such encampments, part of a well-organised network, which included arsenals and a military and religious hierarchy.

I continued along the ridge, grateful that the long climb was over. Although I had not yet covered half of the day's journey, the remainder would be less strenuous. Another thing that pleased me was that the sweat and toil I was experiencing was reducing my waistline!

As if to increase my pleasure the conditions were becoming much brighter and, as I neared the halfway point, the sun was getting into its stride. Its welcome rays revealed a magnificent vista, clearer than that I had experienced at Signal de Bougès, of mile upon mile of mountains stretching into southern Languedoc. I felt I was in the very heart of the Cévennes, enjoying what would probably be some of the finest views of my entire walk. The glory of the region had been truly revealed at last and my disappointment at poor visibility on the summit of Mont Lozère was forgotten.

I could see the ribbon of track that I was following snaking along the crest of the descending ridge, above heather-strewn slopes, before contouring a mountainside in the far distance. As I did so I spied a string of walkers on the track not far beneath me. I felt certain it was my French friends that I had encountered the previous day. This turned out to be correct, for I caught up with them twenty minutes later. They were eating lunch at the side of the track and seemed pleased to see me. I joined them and ate the half of the French stick I had been given earlier, washed down with plenty of water. It was gratifying to be in the company of such friendly people, some of whom offered me food. Despite our language difficulties it was a most pleasant interlude as we sat in glorious sunshine amidst thrilling surroundings.

Some members of the group admitted that they were feeling the strain of the demanding walk and needed more time to recover their strength. They suggested that I carry on as they had no wish to delay me. I asked where they were staying that evening and found it was the hotel at which I had also booked accommodation. With a promise to see them in the hotel bar later, I bade them goodbye and resumed the long descent to Florac.

This took most of the afternoon and was extended by

Florac

nearly an hour, due to my veering off the GR 70 in error in the hills above Florac. Everything had gone well up to that point. I was descending a wriggling track into the yawning valley when I noticed an arrow on the ground, made with pine cones, indicating a path through trees. I had seen many such arrows, normally made with red paint, used as an additional aid to the GR70 waymarkers. Assuming this revealed a short cut, I left the track and set off down the path. It was a wrong move for which I paid the price. Eventually, I joined another track, which, instead of descending began to undulate. Already committed to this route and unwilling to backtrack, I persevered until so much time had elapsed I felt I should have been in Florac. However, the town was nowhere in sight and neither was the valley bottom. At long last the track began to descend, into the wrong valley as it turned out. Instead of seeing Florac beneath me, the village of Bedoues, to the north east of the town, appeared. I was way off my route! Desperation set in and I was determined to reach the bottom of the valley of the Tarnon, my intended destination, without further delay. I took the first available path in that direction and after a hasty decent I emerged onto a road two kilometres from Florac. Cursing my foolishness I followed the road into the valley bottom where it meets the main road into Florac.

A short time later I stood on the bridge overlooking the Tarnon on the outskirts of the town. The tree-lined river flows on a straight course, sandwiched between the main road and the long main street of town. Its surroundings are dramatic with craggy mountaintops rising above the verdant lower slopes of the narrow crevasse. This view provided some consolation for missing the Tarn Gorge and I was convinced it was just as spectacular.

The Tarnon rises near the summit of Mont Aigoual, to the south and flows through Florac to meet the Tarn just to the north of the town. The Tarn Gorge extends westward to Ste Enimie, as the pastor, with whom he had conversed, had informed Stevenson. I learned of a legend relating to a spot in this section of the gorge. On an overhanging rock sit the ruins of a medieval castle high above the tiny village of Castelbouc. This shattered and ghostly ruin is reckoned to be haunted and has become known as the 'castelbouc' (castle of the goat). During the Middle Ages the knight who owned the castle lived a life of extreme self-indulgence whilst his fellow nobles were away risking their lives in the Crusades. When he died through his excesses, his spirit, unable to rest in peace, was forced to roam the crags in the form of a huge goat. This ghastly presence scared off the castle's next owners. Later, a group of bandits, exploiting local fear of the castle and its impregnable position on top of the sixty-metre-high rock, used 'castelbouc' as a hideout.

Gorge du Tarn

Eventually, their terrorising of the neighbourhood became intolerable and they were forcibly evicted. To prevent re-occupation the castle was virtually destroyed four hundred years ago and it has remained a ruin. If you are courageous and willing to risk meeting the goat, the view from the pinnacle is spectacular.

The scenic introduction to Florac put me in a better frame of mind and I forgot my recent troubles. It is ideally situated at the junction of three mountainous regions; the Gorges de Tarn, the Cévennes and Le Grand Causses. Since 1976 it has been the seat of the Cévennes National Park Authority, which has a permanent exhibition. Florac has been described as a 'perfect little town' and its ambiance supports that view. The main street is modern and spacious at the northern end with impressive buildings and tree-sprinkled gardens lining it. At the southern end, in the old town, the tall, more aged buildings crowd in on each side and it becomes more or less as Stevenson would have known it.

The town is a magnet for tourists, but in earlier times that was not the case. A young pastor, Paul Arnal, a keen potholer, in addition to his faith, was anxious to contribute towards the development of tourism in the region. In 1894 he created the Club Cévenole in order to promote its attributes. It became an energetic association and amongst its activities was the publicising of *Voyage de Stevenson*, a translation of *Travels with a Donkey in the Cévennes,* carried out by the Cévenole, Moulharac in 1901. Arnal and his colleagues believed that Stevenson's account of his travels in the region would inspire people to visit.

An example of the minister's compassion and enterprise was his devotion to the reconciliation of Catholicism and Calvinism (Protestantism).

As I walked through the town I gazed above its buildings to the rocky pinnacles of Le Causse Méjean, a massive wall of tufa that dominates Florac. The rock is composed of layers of solidified sediment derived from a nearby spring. This rock was used for the construction of the chateau, now in ruins, perched on the Causse. This fortification has a long history and was rebuilt in 1652 after the Wars of Religion.

During the Revolution it was used for storing salt. Bars on the windows and cell doors of the ruin are a reminder of its use as a prison after being sold to the State in 1810.

The only blot on the town was the sight of a garish modern building in its centre. Its plain box-like shape and ugly façade seem quite out of keeping with its surroundings.

I was much more impressed by the hotel where I was due to stay. In fact, it occupied two buildings, connected by attractive gardens. As I approached the complex along its impressive drive I knew that my overnight stay in Florac would be as rewarding as the town itself. This proved to be the case, for it proved very comfortable and was efficiently run. After meeting the French party in the bar, as arranged, I enjoyed a delightful meal in their company.

CHAPTER EIGHT

FLORAC TO ST. GERMAIN DE CALBERTE

A day's walk of twenty-nine kilometres (eighteen miles) lay ahead as I left the hotel to purchase supplies for the journey. Who should I meet but the two elderly Frenchmen? On this occasion I was not offered half of a French stick! The man who had given it to me was not in a very good state and declared he was exhausted. Unfortunately, I never encountered them again, and was unable to see how he fared.

On my way out of town I was given a reminder that the Camisard conflict was not forgotten in the region. A sign above the door of a store dealing in the sale and exchange of second hand goods declared 'Au Troc Cévenole' (Cévenole Exchange).

Another piece of evidence to this effect can be seen in the village of Magistavols that lay just off my day's route. It is a plaque in memory of 'Spirit Séguier,' leader of the local Camisards, who was born there in 1647. It indicates that he was burnt alive on the 12th August 1702, in Pont de Montvert, and the plaque was placed there to commemorate the 250th anniversary of the brutal event.

The weather was continuing its improvement and I was looking forward to travelling through the valley of the Mimente, the first section of my day's walk. It is akin to the impressive valley of the Tarn and Stevenson found it equally appealing. He gave it a favourable 'write-up,' and chose to camp overnight on its slopes.

I crossed the bridge over the Tarnon, bade goodbye to pleasant Florac and entered the valley of the Mimente. The GR 70 is never far from the road and river during its distinctly meandering passage through the valley and I chose to stick to the road for the initial part of my traverse. This meant that my progress would be quicker, for it hugs the valley bottom and eliminates the frequent rises and falls of the GR 70 on the steep slopes.

Stevenson heard the periodic sound of herdsman's horns during his passage, but these have been replaced by the noise of modern traffic coursing through the valley along what is the main road between Florac and Alais.

I met the only traveller that I was to encounter that day, a cyclist, who enlivened the rather tedious road-walking, for he stopped and dismounted, seemingly eager for a chat. He spoke rapidly, typical of the French, and I could not decipher what he was saying. When I pointed this out to him he switched to perfect English. It transpired he was an itinerant rover, which was borne out by his belongings that were festooned on his cycle. His weather-beaten features conveyed a life in the open air and he seemed content with his nomadic existence. Born in Le Puy, he had received a good education and practiced as a lawyer before becoming dissatisfied with what he considered a cloistered existence. Determined to live a more satisfying life, he switched to one on the open road and had never regretted it.

When I explained that I was following in Stevenson's footsteps, his eyes lit up. Ah! he said. 'He and I are similar beings, although his travels were on foot and mine by cycle. I wish I had his talent for words. I would make myself a fortune recording my adventures,' he joked. It appeared that he had read much of Stevenson's writings and he was very familiar with the Camisards and their troubles. He told me of the plaque in Magistavols that he had recently passed through and bemoaned the fate of 'Spirit Séguier.' 'His slaying of du Chayla was wrong, but he rid the land of a tyrant,' he declared.

I asked the man where he was heading. 'Wherever the spirit moves me,' was his reply. A remarkable person, I reckoned.

My tramping over tarmac was eased by close views of the majestic Mimente. It travels hand in hand with the winding road, alternately foaming as it rushes over dramatic cataracts, or crystal clear as it traverses deep channels between layered rocky walls.

I passed through the villages of La Salle Prunette and St. Julien d'Arpaon. The latter stands in the shadow of a ruined chateau that dominates this part of the valley. Here I joined the dismantled railway that follows a dramatic route along a shelf on the valley side overlooking the river. Despite

St. Julien d'Arpaon

protests from the local population the railway closed in 1968 and the rails were removed, even though plans were in hand to make it a tourist attraction.

The disused bed of the railway forms an excellent walking track that passes over spectacular viaducts and offers splendid views over the river beneath. The only slight drawback to my seven-kilometre traverse of the railway was its passage through three dark tunnels, where you become enveloped by an eerie silence. (I must contact those responsible for the maintenance of the GR 70 to suggest they install lighting in them!) Stevenson would not have been able to take advantage of this convenient railway track, for it had not been constructed when he passed along the valley. It must have been quite a feat of civil engineering to create the ledge, on which the railway ran, from solid rock. The viaducts skirt sheer cliffs, adding drama to the line and the tunnels would have required the blasting of many tons of the layered metamorphic schist.

The building of the railway, intended to link Florac with

ICI EST NÉ
VERS 1647
PIERRE-ESPRIT SÉGUIER
PREMIER CHEF DES CAMISARDS
BRULÉ VIF LE 12 AOUT 1702
AU PONT-DE MONTVERT
250 ᵐᵉ ANNIVERSAIRE
MUSÉE DU DESERT. 1952

Tablet in Memory of 'Spirit Séguier'

the Nimes-Paris main line, was completed within three years, between 1906 and 1909. During this period the valley was swarming with construction workers, singing songs of the Camisard uprising as they toiled. In November 1908 the first locomotive arrived in Florac, not by rail, but by road! It was drawn by twelve horses and eight pairs of oxen.

During its working life the railway transported miners, local peasants, the first holidaymakers and also minerals and wood. The line must have been a lifeline to the people of the secluded valley of the Mimente.

Beside the disused railway, beyond St. Julien d'Arpaon lie the remains of the ancient Mine de Bougès. An old cottage, still inhabited, stands above the gaunt ruins that probably provided the only work for the people of the valley, other than farming and logging.

I continued my passage through the meandering valley to pass beneath the tiny hamlet of Croses–Bas before striking out for Cassagnas that stands some two kilometres from the GR 70. On the approach to Cassagnas I reached a campsite, beyond which stands the former station, now the Robert Louis Stevenson restaurant. I could think of much better memorials to him, for this is an ugly modern monstrosity, quite out of keeping with its pleasant wooded surroundings. As I surveyed the disappointing building I had a decision to make. Should I visit Cassagnas and lose over an hour, or carry on along the GR70? I knew I had an imminent hard climb out of the valley, which persuaded me to forgo Cassagnas. I was disappointed, for I had looked forward to visiting the village where Stevenson dined at the inn. However, I would not have found the hostelry, for the last hotel-restaurant closed in 2002. Another spot I would have searched for if time had allowed is the cave in the vicinity used as an arsenal by the Cévenoles. Cassagnas was staunchly Protestant and one of the main seats of Camisard resistance, hence the arsenal. Not only was it used for storing weapons, as Stevenson relates, but also for housing corn, food and the sick and wounded. Another reminder of the Camisard's struggle is the monument, erected in their memory, high in the Forest of Fontmort that I was due to pass through on my route.

During the Second World War Cassagnas was a centre of the Resistance movement. One of its foremost members, Hans Mosch, a German political refugee, was killed by the Waffen SS in 1944. A simple roadside cross bears his name, his photograph and the inscription, 'Died for Liberty.'

I crossed the Mimente by the Pont du Croupatas and began a protracted ascent of the thickly wooded valley side. So steep was the slope that the rugged track wound back and forth like a writhing snake. During the initial two kilometres of the ascent I actually progressed a mere half a kilometre! Imagine my consternation as, tired and hot, I passed the ruined hamlets of La Revolte and Les Boubaux, neither of which I was inclined to explore. No wonder they are deserted, I reckoned, if their inhabitants had this climb to negotiate!

At last the stony track levelled out, but the enveloping forest shut out any outlook. This was disappointing, for Stevenson had breathtaking views from here that he considered the finest of his journey. He saw the Gulf of

Lyon; all I saw was the track weaving through the chestnut trees ahead of me. I had one consolation, however, as the path he was following disappeared and he was obliged to leave Modestine and go in search of a track, or road. As luck would have it he met a lone aged shepherd, who directed him to the nearest thoroughfare. Stevenson wondered how the man had reached the lofty ridge on which they were standing. Jokingly, he wondered if the man could be a relic from the battle that took place nearby at Plan de Fontmort, many years ago and had wandered ever since, like Rip Van Winkle, upon the mountains. The conflict was between the local legion of Camisards, led by Séguier, and the hated dragoons. Tragically, many Camisards lost their lives, a goodly number being slain by 'the Armenian sabre of Poul,' as Stevenson wrote.

The Plan de Fontmort lay deep in the forest ahead of me and it took a good half-hour of toil on that hot afternoon to reach it. In the vicinity stands a monument, erected in 1887 on the centenary of the Edict of Nantes, to commemorate the fallen Camisards. The inscription reads, *'A l'occasion du Centenaire de l'edit de tolerance les fils des Huguenots ont sur le theatre des anciens combats eleve ce monument a la paix religieuse. Et a la memoire des martyrs, 1887.'*

Unfortunately, I was unable to read the above, for I could not find the monument. It lay just off of my map and the GR 70. Despite leaving the path to search for it, the obelisk remained hidden. I wandered a veritable maze of paths in the vicinity, but called off my search in case I lost my way and suffered the conjectured fate of the shepherd that Stevenson met!

I returned to the GR 70 at the point where it swings to the east and is joined by the GR 7 and the GR 67 with which it keeps company for the next two kilometres. A short time later the ground to my right began to fall away dramatically and the trees receded. I could now enjoy a view similar to that experienced by Stevenson as I gazed over steep slopes of schist strewn with patches of grass, heather and broom. Beyond, line upon line of hills was visible in the radiant sunshine and I could detect Mont Aigoual, the former bastion of another Camisard chief, in the far distance.

Forest near Col de la Pierre Plantee

My vantage-point marked the beginning of an inspiring ridge walk to Col de la Pierre Plantee on which there are signs of ancient burial sites, and possibly, ritual. For example, on a rocky ledge stands a menhir and a dolmen, the latter being a smaller version of the one near Le Thort, a remnant of Megalithic habitation. The Megaliths, a peaceful Mediterranean race, arrived on these shores roughly 5,000 years ago. They established settlements, practiced their religion and built elaborate tombs for their dead. Many examples of their work can be found in Cornwall, such as the massive quoits and burial chambers.

I found another illustration of their presence farther along the track, indicated on the map as 'Sepulture à coffre' (Burial chest) where I found what seemed like a small tomb, without a cover, which could possibly have been made for a for a child.

After a period of intermittently enjoying unrestricted vistas and being enveloped by trees I reached Col de la Pierre Plantee, situated at 890metres (2,920feet), where

St. Germain de Calberte

there is a small reservoir and another menhir. I took a break at this point before the last lap of my day's journey to Le Serre de la Can, a hamlet adjacent to St. Germain de Calberte, where I was due to stay the night.

Just as during the latter stages of the previous day's walk, I ran into difficulties, which added time and distance to a gruelling day. The forest tracks became more numerous and confusing, a situation made worse by the absence of GR 70 waymarks. I backtracked several times before becoming so exasperated I was reduced to asking for directions from a family whose parked car I came upon. They proved extremely helpful, for I found them waiting for me after a further kilometre, on a wide bend in the track. The lady pointed to a narrow unmarked path through trees that I would certainly have ignored, indicating that it gave access to the hotel. She was absolutely correct, for I found my accommodation a short time later as I emerged from the mantle of trees. I mentally thanked the family, for they saved me from a protracted search.

The hotel looked very impressive, standing amidst a modern leisure complex, which includes a sports centre, outdoor swimming pool and chalets. Three mature stone pyramids stand near the hotel, unidentified and strangely out of keeping with the modern site.

My enthusiasm for the place began to wane when I entered the strange confines of the hotel. I discovered later that the building was designed by an eccentric. Incorporated into it is a tower and I was led up its punishing spiral staircase to the top floor by a very energetic young female receptionist. She climbed the steps so quickly that it took all my strength to keep up with her. She ushered me into a small, very basic room, without a toilet and left as smartly as she had climbed the exhausting stone steps. When I had recovered my breath I opened a tiny window to let in some fresh air and, being right at the top of the tower, I felt like Rapunsal, but my hair was too short to let down!

A little later I suffered 'trial by shower,' in a roughly three-foot square cubicle. In these contrivances your frustration knows no bounds as you struggle to get the water to the right temperature. Having achieved this at last, it stubbornly refuses to remain so. Add the painful task of trying to wash without banging elbows and knees on the controls or the structure itself and you have the Chinese torture that I assume countless people suffer in these claustrophobic boxes.

I descended my ivory tower to discover that I was the only guest that evening. If so, why had I been banished to the top floor of the tower? Did they expect me to abscond without paying the bill? The receptionist had disappeared and I came face to face with this intimidating mountain of a man behind the bar, who looked like Joe Stalin. He was casually dressed in T-shirt and trousers that immersion in water would have done no harm to, but he was jovial enough. Unfortunately, he struggled with my inadequate French and he named me, 'English.' I don't know what his position was, or if the hotel employs a chef. If they do, he was sorely missed, for 'Joe' offered to cook a meal for me, which turned out be one of the worst I have ever experienced. When he suggested a salad starter, followed by steak and potatoes with raspberry tart as a sweet, it sounded quite acceptable.

Whist we were discussing my meal, several of 'Joe's' family turned up, ordered drinks and began what turned out to be a lengthy social gathering in the bar. They were the only people I encountered that evening. I was shown into the large dining room and left on my own to await 'Joe's' culinary delights. The finished article was much different to my expectation. The salad was thrown together, but adequate, the main course, a total disaster. Whatever beast the steak came from was either a skinny athletic animal or had seen better days. It was fatty, grisly and tough as old boots, but excellent exercise for my jaw. So much so, I thought the evening would be over before I reached the sweet course. The potatoes were prepared, French-style, diced and in the form of fishcakes, dripping in fat and totally inedible. Why, did I not complain, I hear you ask? Would you wish to insult a burly Frenchman by decrying his cooking? Despite his bonhomie, 'Joe' looked as though he could easily turn nasty.

I gave some feeble excuse for leaving most of the main course and was relieved when he raised no objection. He can't adulterate the sweet, I reckoned. It was passable, but taken straight from the fridge and far from fresh. To round off the most unsatisfying meal, the milk for the coffee was on the turn.

CHAPTER NINE

ST. GERMAIN DE CALBERTE TO ST. JEAN DU GARD

'Joe' was the only person to be seen the next morning and was still wearing the same attire, which did not surprise me. He had prepared breakfast and, true to form, the single available croissant was cold and burnt on the bottom, so I made do with toast.

Today was to be the final one of my journey and I was looking forward to reaching St. Jean du Gard. However, plenty of tough walking remained although my itinerary declared it to be a mere twenty-one kilometres (thirteen miles).

The weather was set fair on my departure. I was not sorry to be leaving the strange hotel, it being no surprise that I was the only person staying the previous evening. So much more could be made of the place, I felt. It was in a fine location and there appeared plenty of activities to be enjoyed in the complex.

I returned to the GR 70 and began a short woodland walk downhill to nearby St. Germain de Calberte. Frequently emerging from the trees, I enjoyed splendid retrospective views of the scattered buildings of Le Serre de la Can nestling on the green terraced hillside amidst garlands of chestnuts. I could also just make out the tower and turret of the ancient Chateau de St. Pierre emerging from the tree-shrouded distant slopes. It dates from medieval times and has been in the course of restoration for the last thirty-five years by a family of goldsmiths of Paris.

The area was in darkness when Stevenson made this descent and he would have missed the beauty of his surroundings. All he encountered was the sound of a woman singing a sad love song not far away and he wished that he could have joined in to comfort her.

It was late in the evening when Stevenson arrived in St. Germain de Calberte and he was not well received at the inn. The landlady was busy putting her children to bed and did not welcome his intrusion. By contrast I saw the quiet, but enchanting village at its best. The morning shadows were receding under an already powerful sun as I wandered its quaint winding streets. I imagined that this would have been how Stevenson saw it the morning after his arrival and that little had changed between our respective visits. He found it one of the most enjoyable places he had ever visited and I could appreciate his joy, for I counted it one of the highlights of my journey. To me it was not only the attractiveness of the village, but also its lovely situation. It stands on a ledge amidst inviting chestnut groves and the views down the verdant valley beneath and to the tree-clad hills beyond gladden the eye.

The place was beginning to come alive and several people were visiting the few shops the village possessed. I called in the boulangerie to purchase food for the final day. Lounging behind the counter were two gendarmes chatting to the pretty girl who served me. I reckoned crime must be at a premium in this sleepy community.

Continuing my exploration I became filled with admiration for the charming old buildings, the foremost being the Catholic Church where Abbé du Chayla lies in his tomb. I was anxious to see his last resting-place, where he was brought on the day after his demise, but unfortunately the church door was locked. The building stood in stony silence, but things would have been much noisier in this little Catholic enclave when the tyrant was laid to rest. As Stevenson points out, the funeral service was rudely interrupted with the news that 'Spirit Séguier' was approaching and pandemonium set in as the congregation and the priest fled.

It seems strange that the people of the village remained staunch Catholics at that time, surrounded as they were by legions of Camisards. They must have been deeply rooted in their faith. Proof that things are different today is provided by the memorial to the local Cévenoles. It stands beside the Protestant chapel on a prominent shelf overlooking the dramatic gorge below, a reminder that Protestant and Catholic now live together in harmony. It comprises a simple pile of stones with the naked figure of a man placing a stone on top. Contrary to its rustic appearance it is a recent addition to the village, for it was erected in the late nineteen nineties.

A Windswept Chateau

Stevenson attracted a great deal of interest as he walked through the village, becoming like the 'Pied Piper' with a band of excited children following in his wake. As he relates, in order to escape this attention he took refuge on a terrace above the village and began to sketch the surrounding chestnuts, endeavouring to capture the natural beauty of their foliage.

Happily, I was allowed to leave the place without attracting an entourage. The villagers are now so used to walkers tramping through on Le Chemin de Stevenson that they are hardly given a second glance.

The temperature was rising with a vengeance as I continued on what would be the easiest section of the day's walk, a gradual descent to St. Etienne Vallée Française. Initially, I followed a winding forest track, which contours the valley side of the Gardon de St. Germain, to Pont de Burgen. The watercourse is one of several in the area with the name of Gardon and it unites with other Gardons before flowing into the Gardon de St. Jean as it heads for my

One of Numerous Ancient Crosses found on the Journey

ultimate destination, St. Jean du Gard.

This was followed by two kilometres of road-pounding along the D984 that led me to the interesting village of St.Etienne Vallée Française. It is a mixture of quaint old buildings and considerable new development. All of its properties are well maintained and many of them were brightly painted, their white walls gleaming in the sunshine. Surrounded by several such dwellings, in a little square, stands the war memorial, not as grand as some I had passed, but just as meaningful. A noticeable feature of my journey was the first-rate condition of the cemeteries and memorials I encountered. They have obviously been well cared for and are another indication of the remembrance of past conflicts and sacrifice by the people of the Cévennes.

The village contains several shops, which were all closed for the afternoon by the time I arrived, but a welcoming café was open. It provided the opportunity to rest and remove the sweat from my brow. Whilst I was enjoying a refreshing drink in the sunshine I noticed two cyclists, a young couple, looking in my direction from an adjacent table. I assumed I appeared a weary looking and overheated Englishman, suffering in the sweltering heat. However, they smiled and gave a friendly wave. Shortly afterwards, as they were leaving, they came over to me and asked how I was faring. I explained that I was on the final lap of Le Chemin de Stevenson and was looking forward to reaching St. Jean du Gard. They understood why I should wish to attempt such a long-distance walk, as they themselves loved the countryside of the Cévennes. However, they preferred to tour the region by cycle, believing you can cover the ground more quickly. I mentioned the cyclists I had encountered whilst climbing La Goulet and their problem in dealing with the rough terrain. The couple reckoned that although arduous, such conditions were not too daunting, providing suitable mounts are used. With cheery farewells we parted company and they sped away on their expensive looking cycles.

My gratifying break had lulled me into a false sense of security. I imagined my journey was all but complete and was about to congratulate myself on my achievement. Had I studied my map more thoroughly I would have discovered what lay in wait.

Blissfully unaware of the sting in the tail that was about to be unleashed, I left the café, rejuvenated and eager to reach journey's end. I crossed a shapely bridge over another Gardon and began the final climb of my journey to Col de St.Pierre. What a climb it turned out to be. Two and a half kilometres of tortuous and twisting forest tracks and an ascent of 306 metres! (1,000 feet). My bonhomie disappeared in a cloud of sweat as I toiled up the stony ribbon under a fierce sun.

With lungs heaving and legs protesting I reached a road. A sign indicated it was half a kilometre to the summit, which is a picnic spot and commanding viewpoint. Several cars passed as I approached the col and people stared at me from the comfort of their vehicles, having attained this lofty site without effort.

Stevenson had climbed to the col in the cool of the evening, but it would have been no mean feat. He writes, 'I hurried to the topmost powers of Modestine, for I dearly

An Old Alley in St. Etienne Vallée Française

desired to see the view upon the other side before the day had faded.' If he hurried up that 1,000 feet climb, he has my unbridled admiration!

Night had fallen before he reached the summit and he records, 'The moon was riding high and clear; and only a few grey streaks of twilight lingered in the west. A yawning valley, engulfed in blackness, lay like a hole in created nature at my feet.'

Possibly in celebration, Stevenson and Modestine enjoyed some refreshment in that elevated spot, which was to be their last meal together.

On my arrival at the summit I slumped onto a bench in a convenient shelter, which provided welcome shade. As I began to recover I was joined by a couple who had wandered from their car, parked nearby. 'Hot, isn't it?' the man proffered, after taking one look at my sweltering face. I agreed. 'Have you come far?' he asked. I did not tell him I had walked from Le Monastier. From his appearance, such an admission would probably have produced the same response as that from the man I met in the dining room of the hotel at Le Bleymard. 'From St. Germain de Calberte,' I replied. Even the mention of the day's journey raised the couple's eyebrows. I could tell by their expressions that they could not imagine why someone would wish to walk such a distance.

The col was enveloped by pines, but, as I began my descent towards St. Jean du Gard gaps appeared revealing stunning views over the Department of Gard, which I had just entered. Since just prior to Langogne I had been traversing the Department of Lozère.

Having clambered laboriously to Col de St. Pierre I was now obliged to descend over 396 metres (1,300 feet) into the valley of the Gardon de St. Jean. I had had my fill of forest tracks over the last nine days so I eschewed the GR 70 and decided to follow the road into the valley. To say the former wriggled, was an understatement, but it was surpassed in this respect by the road, typical of those in the Alps.

It was therefore a protracted descent, buoyed by the fact that it was the last gasp of my journey. My progress was

St. Jean du Gard

slowed by the extreme contortions of the road as I approached the scenic Corniche des Cévennes, a striking gorge cut by Louis XIV in pursuit of the Camisards. Despite the delightful views into its depths, I grew tired of observing them repeatedly from different angles as the road snaked hither and thither. I could see the junction of roads I was heading for in the valley bottom for three-quarters of an hour before I actually reached it.

At long last I reached the junction, where I was re-united with the GR 70 that follows the busy D907 road into St. Jean du Gard. My excitement mounted as I covered the final one and a half kilometres to the old town. When I arrived I had taken taken eight hours to cover the supposed thirteen miles from St. Germain de Calberte.

Stevenson records, 'Before ten o'clock we had got in (the inn at St. Jean du Gard) and were at supper; fifteen miles and a stiff hill in little beyond six hours!' In mitigation I did have a lunch-stop and a half-hour break at the café in St. Etienne Vallée Française!

I was not overly impressed by my initial view of St. Jean
du Gard, as I progressed along narrow Grand Rue towards
the town-centre. The tall sombre buildings have a rather run
down feel and many of them look in need of refurbishment.
Its bustling centre is a mixture of old and new. Picturesque
properties mingle with the modern supermarket and
souvenir shops.

In fairness to St. Jean du Gard, my stay in the town was
too short to absorb much of its vibrant activity. It is
renowned for its colourful open-air markets with garments
made from the famous 'Provencal' and distinctive glazed
pottery 'Faience de Moustiers.' The place attracts large
numbers of visitors, judging by the crowds in its heart
during my brief inspection.

The town was also a centre of Protestant resistance
during the Camisard uprising and the name of the local
museum, 'Musée des Vallées Cévenoles' is a reminder of the
conflict. It houses displays of local life that include
furniture, domestic tools, items from the local lace industry
and other trades, including silk spinning. The factory
women performing the latter endured tough working
conditions, indicated by the rules and regulations on
display.

There are several references to Stevenson in St. Jean du
Gard and the most interesting of them was pointed out to
me by a person from Harrogate, which is very close to my
home. Intent on finding the hotel where I was due to stay
the night, I decided to ask for directions and chose this man
who was getting out of his car. It was a bonus to find an
Englishman, especially one who was local to me. I learned
that he knew the area very well, having spent several holidays
in St. Jean du Gard. I happened to mention that I had just
completed Le Chemin de Stevenson and he asked if I had
seen the ring to which Stevenson had tethered Modestine.
This was a reference to the fact that Stevenson had found
Modestine unfit to travel the morning after their arrival in
the town. Eager to reach Alais to collect his mail he
decided to sell her to the highest bidder. Having spread
the word that she was for sale he tethered her to the ring,
whilst he proceeded to bargain with prospective buyers.

I was surprised to find how small the ring was when the man led me to the doorway of a building, to which it was attached, having expected a sturdier object.

Other references to Stevenson include a fountain in his memory and 'Les Jardins de Stevenson,' (a bar and restaurant). Even a cinema, 'Salle Stevenson,' is named after the renowned author and traveller.

The Avenue de la Resistance recalls the town's contribution towards combating the occupation by German forces in World War Two. Nearby, in June1944, a German regiment capitulated to Marceau Lapierre, a local schoolmaster and Resistance leader, and his Maquisards.

The pleasant Gardon de St. Jean, which flows through St. Jean du Gard is spanned by its most dramatic landmark, the Pont du Gard. As beautiful as it is functional, it is a tribute to Roman engineering. The aqueduct was constructed as part of a system to supply fresh water to Nimes, employing aqueducts, trenches and tunnels carved out of solid rock. Its three great tiers of limestone arches are virtually unchanged since its construction. The marks of the original builders can be seen on some of the stones, the largest weighing six tons. It was necessary to build on this monumental scale to ensure it was not damaged or destroyed by the energetic river that can become a raging torrent in winter, capable of sweeping away modern bridges, as it did in 1958. The Roman engineers designed the aqueduct with a slight curve to enable it to withstand a great pressure of water.

On the final evening of my journey I ate in the restaurant adjacent to the hotel where I was staying overnight. I noticed from the menu that Cévenole cuisine was served. This was yet another remembrance of the resistance against religious intolerance. The hotel itself was agreeable and set in pleasant gardens, with a swimming pool right outside the window of my room. I could have opened my window and dived in!

The following morning when I went down for breakfast I encountered several of the party of French walkers, who I had not seen since leaving Florac. Surprisingly, one of them began to speak English, the first time any of their group had done so. I smiled inwardly, for it confirmed my suspicions that many French people who can speak English refrain from doing so, or only divulge the fact if you are making an attempt to converse in their language. We reminisced over our respective experiences during the walk before saying our goodbyes and beginning our homeward journeys.

Stevenson recounted that Modestine, for all her faults had been a constant companion during his expedition and I felt that he had kept company with me during mine. From the constant reminders of his presence I realised that he is probably better known in this area of France than in Britain. Ask anyone from our country who he was and from those who know, the reply will be, 'The man who wrote *Treasure Island*.' Whereas, in the Cévennes the instant reply is, 'Ah, oui! Le Chemin de Stevenson!'

I had fulfilled my ambition to walk in his footsteps and discover how things have changed in this mountainous region during the intervening years. The answer is, very little in the greater part of the Cévennes. Apart from the tourist towns of Florac and St. Jean du Gard its more remote outposts remain virtually untouched by time, the only concession to modernity being the occasional village store, Office de Tourisme and a Cévennes National Park Centre.

Another discovery was the arduous nature of Stevenson's journey. It follows many of the ancient and demanding packhorse roads, what we would term rough tracks. I found the going extremely tough in places, but with a fractious and wilful donkey as your companion, it would have been doubly hard.

INDEX

Sagne-Rousse 15,90
Sahara, the 104
Saloman 61
Saltburn 77
Salve Regina 30,
Seguier, 'Spirit' 43,44,51,57,
61,132,133,135, 137,143
Sepulture a coffre 138
Sete 39
Sharp, Archbishop 41
Signal de Bouges 124,125,126
Sommet de Finiels 117
St. Bees 77
St. Etienne 10
St. Etienne Vallee Francaise 63,
144,145,147,150
St. Flour de Mercoire 89,90,94
St. Germain de Calberte 56,
59,60,61,63,66,132,139,142,
148,149
St. Jean du Gard 60,64,65,
142,145,146,148,149,150,152
St. Julien d' Arpaon 133,134,
135
St. Martin de Fugeres 4,73
St. Pierre, hill of 63,64
Ste-Enimie 53,128
Syria 104

Tarn, Valley of 38,48,51,54
Tour de France 95
*Travels with a Donkey in the
Cevennes* 130
Treasure Island 152

Ussel 5,78,79,81

Valour, Dom Claudius 100
Velay, the 11,83,88
Versailles 12

Vigils, the 102
Vilar, Jean 90
Villefort 35,115
Vivarais 42
Voyage de Stevenson 130

Waffen SS 136
Wainwright 115
Wainwright's Coast to Coast
Walk 77
Wars of Religion 93,130
Waverley Novels 30
William III 45
Wolds Way 77
Wordsworth, William 25
Work of the Propogation of
the Faith 21,43

Yorkshire 77,84
Yorkshire Dales 77